D0195834

The
Girls' Guide
TO

CONQUERING
MIDDLE SCHOOL

Books by Erica & Jonathan Catherman

The Girls' Guide to Conquering Life
The Girls' Guide to Conquering Middle School

Books by Jonathan Catherman

The Manual to Manhood
The Manual to Middle School

The *Girls' Guide* TO

CONQUERING MIDDLE SCHOOL

"DO THIS, NOT THAT"
Advice Every Girl Needs

ERICA CATHERMAN AND JONATHAN CATHERMAN

Revell

a division of Baker Publishing Group
Grand Rapids, Michigan

© 2018 by Erica and Jonathan Catherman

Published by Revell
a division of Baker Publishing Group
PO Box 6287, Grand Rapids, MI 49516-6287
www.revellbooks.com

Printed in the United States of America

All rights reserved. No part of this publication may be reproduced, stored in a retrieval system, or transmitted in any form or by any means—for example, electronic, photocopy, recording—without the prior written permission of the publisher. The only exception is brief quotations in printed reviews.

Library of Congress Cataloging-in-Publication Data
Names: Catherman, Erica, 1975– author.
Title: The girls' guide to conquering middle school : do this, not that advice every girl needs / Erica Catherman and Jonathan Catherman.
Description: Grand Rapids : Revell, 2018. | Includes bibliographical references and index.
Identifiers: LCCN 2018017068 | ISBN 9780800729813 (pbk. : alk. paper)
Subjects: LCSH: Preteen girls—Conduct of life—Juvenile literature. | Teenage girls—Conduct of life—Juvenile literature. | Middle school students—Conduct of life—Juvenile literature. | Preteen girls—Education (Middle school)—Juvenile literature. | Teenage girls—Education (Middle school)—Juvenile literature.
Classification: LCC BJ1651 .C38 2018 | DDC 170.84/2—dc23
LC record available at https://lccn.loc.gov/2018017068

The authors are represented by the literary agency of Books & Such.

18 19 20 21 22 23 24   7 6 5 4 3 2 1

In keeping with biblical principles of creation stewardship, Baker Publishing Group advocates the responsible use of our natural resources. As a member of the Green Press Initiative, our company uses recycled paper when possible. The text paper of this book is composed in part of post-consumer waste.

CONTENTS

INTRODUCTION

*M*iddle school can be like a roller-coaster ride of emotions, friendships, and physical changes. The ups, downs, twists, and turns during this time of life can, at times, overwhelm your senses. Kind of like the odd sensation you get at an amusement park when a ride barrels down the track at Mach speeds into a massive blind drop, followed by two loops, and a stomach-churning corkscrew. Sometimes you feel like you're about to lose your stomach and find yourself screaming uncontrollably. Guess what, girl? Those are totally normal feelings in middle school too. Whether you enjoy the thrill of the ride or absolutely hate the suspense, it's best to embrace the changes and learn some new levels of self-control in order to make the most of the next few years. Who knows, you may actually have a pretty good time in middle school.

Jump from the craziness of an amusement park to the drama of a theater. A poorly performed "drama" can ruin some potential good times in middle school. The poet and author Maya Angelou once said that you may not control all the events that happen to you, but you can decide not to be reduced by them. That's some good advice for middle school too. Drama in middle school can be like tossing fuel onto a fire . . . it explodes. Making much to-do about nothing is the fuel that feeds the fire between people that can blow friendships apart. Try to extinguish the drama by thinking carefully about your actions and words. Here's a good filter: Before you speak, text, or post on social media, *THINK* about what you are about to do or say.

- Is it *TRUE?*
- Is it *HELPFUL?*

- Is it *INSPIRING*?
- Is it *NECESSARY*?
- Is it *KIND*?

This anti-drama filter has been around for years and works pretty well for anyone mature enough to *THINK* before they act.

We're just getting started. This book is all about giving you lots of helpful hints and the kind of "Do This, Not That" advice every girl needs as she grows older. Basically, you want to succeed, and we want you to succeed in conquering middle school. For now, please accept this book as our gift to you because we believe in you. We hope what you read next will help you be and do your very best in middle school and beyond. Good luck, girl, and enjoy your middle school journey!

MIDDLE
SCHOOL

1st DAY

*B*efore you arrive for the first day of middle school, it's best to know a little about what you're stepping into. Here's what you need to know about the first day. At least one-third of the students are new to the building, and they are feeling about the same as you. The older kids are excited to see their friends, so they won't pay much attention to the newbies walking around. The building is bigger, halls are louder, and passing between classes can be like moving through a crazed herd of cats. The truth is, you might get lost once or twice on the first day of school. But don't worry about it because you won't be the only one. A right turn down the wrong hall can send anybody into the land of the lost. If you do find yourself wandering around, don't freak out. Your best plan for getting back on track and heading the right direction is only three steps away.

STEP 1—Ask for directions. The worst thing you can do is keep standing there looking lost.

STEP 2—Get moving. The classroom isn't coming to you, so don't just stand there.

STEP 3—Don't make excuses. When you do finally make it to class, just tell the teacher that you got lost. They'll totally understand when you're honest about a mistake.

Pop Quiz

Q: Where is the school gym?

A: You have no idea, so tape a school map on the inside cover of a master folder. When you get lost, just open the folder, read the map, and find your way to gym class.

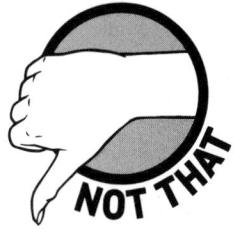

⊚⊚⊚⊚⊚⊚⊚⊚ ABSENCES ⊚⊚⊚⊚⊚⊚⊚⊚

*A*ccording to experts in middle school attendance offices everywhere, there are three legit reasons to be absent from school:

Reason #1, Sick—An infection, affliction, or disorder that can be diagnosed. Symptoms include a high temperature, chunks hurling out of either end of your digestive system, broken bones, or another verifiable illness. NOT sick is when you are faking it.

Reason #2, Emergency—Situations requiring immediate action, like the passing of a family member, your home is damaged in a freak weather storm, or the zombie apocalypse. NOT an emergency is the death of your goldfish, boyfriend breakups, or your favorite jeans didn't get washed due to a false call on that zombie apocalypse thing.

Reason #3, Professional intervention—When serious life or legal needs require outside professional or legal help. These may include, but are not limited to, counseling, court, or a doctor appointment. NOT an intervention includes "doing time" on the beach or a 10-hour therapy session with "Dr. Shopping."

When you are absent for a day or two, return with a parent's or doctor's note with a legitimate explanation of your absence.

True OR False?

The school really doesn't need to know why you were absent.

False. When you are absent for a day or two, return with a parent's or doctor's note with a legitimate explanation for your absence.

ANANNOUNCEMENTS

*E*ach morning a mystical voice from the great beyond will guide you into the school day. Actually, the voice will come from a squawking overhead speaker or live-screen broadcast from a "studio" somewhere in the media center or main office. Either way, the info shared over the school announcements is worth paying attention to if knowing today's lunch menu, the bell schedule, the next awards assembly, or the grade level winning the school-wide fundraiser is important to you. Such information is power, so sit down, listen up, and collect all the news you need to rule the day.

True Story

A pioneer for women in broadcasting, Barbara Walters became the first female co-anchor of a US network evening news program in 1976. Featured nightly on the *ABC Evening News*, Walters earned $1 million a year, which was a first for a female journalist. As one of the most respected journalists in television history, she was celebrated for her interview style and quality, which granted her access to some of the world's most famous and influential people. Listed as one of *TV Guide*'s "50 Greatest TV Stars of All Time," she interviewed movie stars, athletes, heroes, and every US president and first lady from Richard and Pat Nixon through Barack and Michelle Obama.

ASSEMBLIES

*T*he freedom of assembly is an important part of the First Amendment to the United States Constitution. When the Founding Fathers penned the rights of our nation, they stated that the people are allowed peaceful assembly. Never did they imagine packs of savage students swarming in crazed assembly. Pep rallies, awards presentations, talent shows, and guest speakers are all perfect times for the entire school to get together and have some fun. The freedoms students get to experience in assemblies include laughing, learning, clapping, cheering, and being part of stuff like class competitions and fun games. Sleeping, messaging, pushing, pranking, and disrupting an assembly are not freedoms, are not protected, and will not be tolerated. So enjoy the break in the school day, keep the gathering peaceful, and the school will grant you the freedom to assemble in another assembly soon.

To Do in Middle School:

✓ Volunteer to represent your grade in a school assembly class competition.

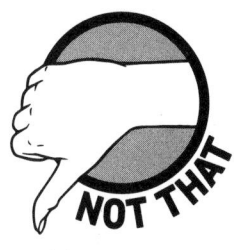

BACKPACKS

*M*ost schools allow students to carry some of their books and class supplies in a midsize backpack. This reduces your need to stop by your locker between every class and makes it easier to carry stuff between home and school. Some girls get the wrong idea about how to use their pack and overstuff it like they are on a yearlong wilderness expedition. Other girls rarely clean out their packs. Old food and sweaty gym clothes quickly go rotten, turning your tote into a putrid canvas petri dish. Your best bet is to pack light and keep it clean. Your back muscles—and the nose of the kid walking behind you—will appreciate it.

Strange but True

Experts recommend a student's backpack weigh no more than 10–20% of their body weight.[1] Yet on average, 6th graders carry backpacks weighing 18.4 pounds. Incredibly, some student packs weighed in as heavy as 30 pounds! What are they stuffing in there? Is math class meeting on the summit of Mt. Everest?

BATHROOM
KEEP IT CLEAN

*T*here are only a few good reasons to visit the room of thrones, and none of them include trashing the place on purpose! Seriously, do what you have to doo-doo, if you need "two," but keep it clean. Flush from your mind any urge to mark a stall door, clog a sink, or scratch the mirrors before returning to class.

Strange but True

Most people "visit" the toilet 6 to 8 times a day. That adds up to an average of 2,555 times a year. At about 2 minutes per stop, the total is just over 85 hours a year of bathroom usage. Divide those 85 hours of toilet time by 24 hours in a day and wow! You spend almost 4 full days per year using the toilet.

BATHROOM
NO LOITERING

*W*hen you tinkle, you sprinkle, and while in the stall, don't touch the wall. The truth is, there's no escaping germ exposure in the bathroom, public or private. This is bad news for germaphobes and grungies alike. With every "use," particles of fecal bacteria go airborne and land on the floor, walls, and your hands. It doesn't even matter if you're a "foot flusher," nobody gets away germ free. To make it simple for all to understand, every time you "go," particles of pee and poo stick to you.

The solution is simple. NO LOITERING! Limit your exposure to toxic toilets by not staying and talking in the bathroom. That and always, always, always wash your hands before leaving.

And PLEASE use soap!

Just Joking

You never really appreciate what you've got until it's gone.

Toilet paper is a good example.

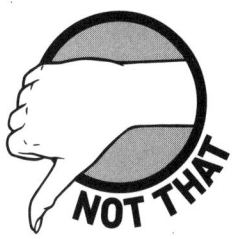

BODY ODOR

*I*magine raising your hand to ask the teacher for a bathroom pass. Suddenly your nose picks up the foul scent of body odor. In horror you realize the pungent perfume is your own armpit aroma. But it's too late. Before the recoil of your arm can close the pit door, an invisible stink cloud has escaped into the air.

"Who will smell me?" you ask yourself.

"The cute boy to my right? Please no!" you beg in a silent prayer.

"Maybe nobody will notice," you hope in vain.

But then you hear it. The boy sitting directly behind you fakes an attention-getting gag as he holds his nose and points in your general direction.

Rewind . . .

There's no need to sweat it. You can raise your hand high with the sweet smell of confidence if you simply shower daily and apply a few swipes of antiperspirant or deodorant to your clean, dry pits. Who knows whose nose will thank you first—yours or the people sitting next to you?

How To . . .
Apply Deodorant or Antiperspirant

Preparation—After showering, dry your armpits.

STEP 1—*Remove cap from deodorant.* Peel off any product seal from the stick of antiperspirant or deodorant.

STEP 2—*Raise one arm.* Lift your arm over your head to expose your open, dry armpit.

STEP 3—*Apply the deodorant.* Swiping up and down in even strokes, apply the deodorant to the skin in your armpit. Repeat under your other arm. Two or three strokes should ensure complete coverage. Too much and people will smell your deodorant before they see you.

STEP 4—*Dry time.* Before putting on a shirt, allow a minute for the deodorant to dry so it won't leave a visible mark on your clothing.[2]

BOOK REPORTS

You are but one girl, writing one paper, in a class of 20 students, all with the same assignment. Your teacher is but one person, grading each paper, from 20 students, all with different perspectives. How will the teacher ever know if you truly read the book? It's just so much easier to skim a few pages, rephrase the book's description, and search the internet for some "ideas" that can be copied, cut, and pasted. Well, believe it or not, teachers know the difference. Maybe it's because they are trained professionals with a degree and official certificate to teach the very class requiring a book report. Maybe it's because they've read way more papers than you'll ever write, and they can smell a false report in the ink. Your best plan is to do the right thing and actually read the book. Think ahead, pace out the pages, take notes, and draft a real report that reflects what you discovered. Who knows? You might just surprise yourself and enjoy the read.

Looking Back

Writing a book report takes time and attention to detail. I found it helpful to first make an outline of what was required in the book report and then add in details to complete the report. Use your own words to build detail, and be sure to cite your sources and references. Then edit, edit, edit . . . yes, at least three times!

—Erica Catherman

BOY FRIENDS

*I*f all the students in your middle school were to gather in the gym, about half of the kids would be girls and half would be boys. Some of the girls standing around might still think guys are loud, lazy, and lacking, and it's lame to be friends with them. Really, girls? Are we still in the 3rd grade here? Spoiler alert: Cooties aren't real and having a friend who's a boy doesn't make him your boyfriend. Friends become friends because they like the same stuff, do the same things, and can trust each other. Girls like sports. Boys like sports. Girls like video games. Boys like video games. Girls like food. Boys like food. Girls like movies. Boys like movies. This means your opportunity to make friends in middle school can and should be a good mix of both girls and boys.

 Quote

"I like us as friends because you join in on my weirdness."

—Anonymous

BRAGGING

*I*t's not bragging if you actually did it," many girls say proudly.

Yeah, but how many times do you need to tell us you did it? Once is cool. Twice is good. Three times or more and now you're boasting. If you're really that good, then others will talk about you, for you. Try this instead. Be interested in other people's interests and accomplishments first. Then when they feel understood and appreciated, they just might ask you about your accomplishments.

Just Joking

A young woman sitting next to an older woman brags, "I have over 100 friends on social media that I've never met." The older woman looks at the younger woman and says, "When I was young we called them imaginary friends."

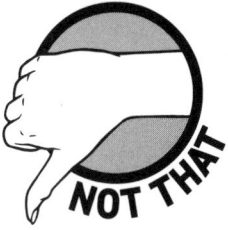

BRUSH YOUR TEETH

*E*verybody likes a friendly smile. Go ahead and show us your pearly whites. Your chiclets, your fangs. Most adults' mouths hold 32 naturally off-white teeth. You may still lose a few in middle school, but basically the tusks in your trap are the ones you'll want to keep for life. This means brushing your teeth every morning and evening, at least. Brushing *with* toothpaste for about two minutes removes food particles and plaque and helps prevent tartar, gum disease, and halitosis. Hal-i-to-sis is the technical term for bad breath from a dirty mouth. Breathing out of a dirty mouth is also called stank, yack chat, and the breath-o-death. Failing to brush your teeth produces a smell that will tell the people you are talking with, "No, I didn't pass gas, I just exhaled in your general direction." So give your grin a good brushing a few times a day. Your mouth—and noses everywhere—will thank you.

True OR False?

The tongue is the strongest muscle in the body.

False. The tongue is not just one muscle; it's actually made up of a team of eight separate muscles. This fun fact disqualifies it from all future single-muscle competition. The hardest working muscle in the body is the heart. Yet, fail to scrub your tongue while brushing your teeth, and your death breath might just give somebody a heart attack.

BUS
TAKE YOUR SEAT

In kindergarten you learned a simple rhyme that went something like this:

> The wheels on the bus go round and round,
>   round and round,
>   round and round,
> The wheels on the bus go round and round,
>   all through the town!

In middle school you'll want to avoid learning a similar song that goes like this:

> The bus driver's head spins round and round,
>   round and round,
>   round and round,
> The bus driver's head spins round and round,
>   when you don't SIT DOWN . . . and zip your lip!

Consider the bus a mobile extension of the school. The good behavior your teachers expect of you in class is also expected of you on the bus. So take your seat, face forward, talk quietly, and always be nice to the bus driver. If someone else is not seated and continually bothering you, don't put up with it. Tell them to stop. If they don't stop, ask the bus driver, a parent, or a teacher for help.

True OR False?

The bus driver has no real authority to discipline misbehaving riders. Basically, what happens on the school bus stays on the school bus.

False. Misbehavior on a school bus can result in suspension of riding privileges, ISS (in-school suspension), and even criminal charges.

BUS

WASTE NOT, WANT NOT

*T*he school bus is not a rolling garbage can. Nobody wants to sit on a bus, period. Absolutely nobody wants to ride in a trashed bus littered with crushed wrappers, ripped paper, old gym shoes, and the rumor of a live rodent named Whiskers that's infected with rabies. So keep your trash to yourself. Keep whatever you bring on the bus *off* the floor, and take it with you when you get off the bus.

Just Joking

What's the difference between a garbage truck and a school bus?

One makes frequent curbside stops, is crammed with bags, and smells bad. The other is a garbage truck.

CAR RIDERS

*T*he car rider pick-up line at your school shares one thing in common with its distant cousin the fast-food drive-through line. Both are intended to move cars through a line to a designated point, make a pickup, and speed away in chase of the next commitment in the day. The difference is how long this exchange takes. Drive-through lines have a goal of getting customers in, served, and out in just a couple of minutes. Whereas the school's car rider line looks more like downtown Los Angeles traffic during rush hour. Parents waiting for students to be released pass the time by snacking, reading, texting, sleeping, and checking on social media. Yet both the business drive-through and chauffeur-like parents must focus on the same goal. Drive in, pick up, and drive out again safely and as quickly as possible.

So do your part and be ready to go when it's your turn to get picked up. Be safe and be quick about it. This way the rest of your day can get started as fast as possible.

Just Joking

Why was the frog waiting at the bus stop?

Because her car got toad.

CELL PHONE

*T*he major organs you need to maintain a happy and healthy life include the heart, lungs, kidneys, liver, intestines, and a bunch of other very important and equally odd-looking body parts. Missing from the list of vital parts is what many girls consider a required lifeline to their daily survival—the cell phone. Contrary to popular belief, lacking access to a mobile device will not send you to the emergency room nor to the top of the tech transplant list. The truth is, when school rules or class codes exclude cell service, you'll survive. Power it off and put it away, before it gets confiscated.

Strange but True
In 1983 the first mobile phone in the US cost a mere $4,000.

CHEATING

*C*heating is easy and for the lazy in life. Thinking the teacher is "dumb" and won't catch you doesn't make the teacher a fool. Instead it shines a light on the fact that you have been trusted with far more than is deserved. Instead of sinking low by cheating, hold your head high and try something a bit more challenging. Build your character on the foundation of honesty, truth, and integrity. You'll feel stronger, stand taller, and be smarter for it.

Ask a Middle School Survivor

Q: What happens if a teacher catches a student cheating?

A: When a teacher catches a student cheating, they usually take them aside to talk and give them a zero grade. If it happens more than once, the student is often sent to the office.

Maya C., from Washington

CLOTHING STYLE

Stand out or blend in—the choice is yours. The style of clothes you choose can make an outward statement of the inward you. Many girls in middle school end up dressing a lot alike, and that's okay. Some girls like the athletic look and wearing basically the same styles as the friends they walk beside. Others will choose a more unique style and try to match their hair color to their thrift store shoes. Some girls will choose an outfit one day that is totally different than the way they dressed the day before, and that's perfectly fine. You will see girls wearing everything from sci-fi printed T-shirts to an iron-pressed blouse, from Sharpie-designed canvas shoes to polished leather boots. From glamor to grunge. Unless there is a standard uniform all students must wear every day, you can expect to see about every style the school's dress code will allow. So experiment with the looks you like and wear each with pride. Just remember, clothes look best when they are not imprinted with wrinkles, are clean both to the eye and nose, and are appropriate for school.

 Quote

"Clothes won't change the world. The women who wear them will."[3]

—Anne Klein

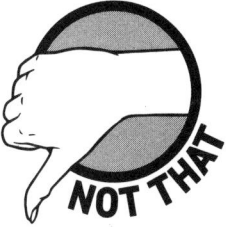

COMMUNICATION

ⓒⓒⓒⓒⓒⓒⓒ **COMMUNICATION** ⓒⓒⓒⓒⓒⓒⓒ

Communication is a numbers game, and you want to win this game. To win you'll need to manipulate the math. Don't freak out. It's easy. To communicate your way to a win with teachers, coaches, and your parents, do the math so your communication equals 100%:

55% body language = Face people, look them in the eye, and smile.

38% tone of voice = Speak clearly and be respectful—no sarcasm.

7% words = Choose your words carefully and stay away from extreme descriptions like "always" or "never," "everybody" and "nobody."

How To . . .
Show You Are Listening in Class

Sit up. Sitting up communicates that you're alert and engaged.

Listen up. Listening to your teacher and other students is a good way to make them feel like what they have to say is important.

Ask questions. Teachers like it when you ask them questions. The trick is to know the right kind of questions to ask:

- **Rule #1**—Ask good questions and expect good answers.
- **Rule #2**—Ask lame questions and you'll get lame answers. (FYI . . . lame questions are intended to distract, disturb, and force the teacher off topic.)
- **Rule #3**—Ask no questions and you'll get no answers.

Nod your head. Teachers are really good at reading nonverbal communication. By nodding your head, it lets them know you are getting what they are teaching.

Track the teacher. To track your teacher means that when they move from one side of the classroom to the other, you keep watching them as they teach. (See "Track the Teacher.")

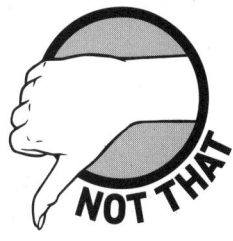

CRYING

*C*rying in middle school is an emotional subject. Some people say girls need to let their feelings show by getting it all out with a good cry. Others recommend girls need to toughen up and bottle it up. What's clear is the average girl sheds tears about 3.75 times a month, for about six minutes per cry.[4] These tears range from, "No I'm not crying. I've just got something in my eye," to full-on "get that girl a box of tissues" sobbing . . . or the "ugly cry." One girl might cry because she just compound-broke her leg in a soccer game, while another cries from embarrassment when her "How to Apply Makeup" video is tagged #clownface, #epicfail, and #needsapressurewasher.

If and when you do cry is somewhat up to you, yet keep this thought in mind: Gone are the elementary school days of tears over spilled milk or lost pencils. The middle school rules are simple. If you didn't get your homework done, there's no crying. If you forgot the field trip permission slip again, there's no crying. If it's the last day before your BFF-since-first-grade moves across the country, some tears may be in order. If you just learned a beloved grandparent has passed away, the tears will flow. If you do feel like a cry is about to happen at school, go talk with your class advisor or school counselor. They'll work to assist you through whatever you're wrestling with, and for sure they can spare a tissue or two.

True OR False?

Only humans shed tears.

False. All animals with backbones—or vertebrae—shed tears. Humans are the only ones thought to shed emotional tears, although elephants have been reported to shed tears when they lose another elephant or are in grief.[5]

⊙⊚⊙⊚⊙⊚⊙⊚ CYBERBULLIES ⊚⊙⊚⊙⊚⊙⊚⊙

*A*lmost everybody is digitally connected today. Wired or wireless, a streaming virtual feed of data is available anytime, from anywhere, between any people. This means flesh-and-bone bullies can make the leap to cyber cruelty with a simple click, post, or stream. Like a virus, digital bullies attack with a text, pic, or tag. They rain down the hurt from the cloud of pain in their life. Selfishly, they are trying to raise themselves up by putting others down with posts or texts about something hurtful, mean, or divisive, or something they think is "funny." To keep digital bullies from "caching" in on your story, do your best to follow these digital life do's and don'ts:

1. Do be careful who you friend, follow, and like online.
2. Don't believe everything you find online.
3. Do a screen capture when a bully strikes and share the evidence with a trusted adult like a parent, teacher, youth group leader, or school administrator.
4. Don't reply to offensive messages or retaliate.
5. Do be filled with integrity and always guard both your digital and analog life.

True OR False?

Life online isn't the same as real life, so digital bullying isn't the same as physical bullying.

False. Cyberbullying is real and very illegal. Online bullies can face arrest and prosecution because all 50 states have bullying laws that include harassment by electronic means that threatens another person's physical well-being.[6] The nationwide trend is toward greater accountability for bullying in general, both in school and off campus. Middle school students have been arrested for cyberbullying and charged with harassment, felony aggravated stalking, and even an offense against a computer system for unauthorized access, which is a felony.

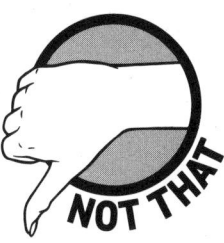

DANCES

*N*o less than two dozen recording artists have released songs titled "Dance Like Nobody's Watching." Not bad advice, if nobody's watching! The girls who take dance lessons growing up usually have a pretty easy time making it look simple on the dance floor. Those of us not so talented might find dancing around others a challenge. It doesn't matter if you have two left feet or own a pair of ballet pointe shoes, you should be able to have a great time at middle school dances. It's really all about hanging out with your friends and having fun. Don't sit around doing nothing! Get up, get down, cut loose, get in the groove, step to the beat, and dance like nobody's watching!

Strange but True

A three-hour ballet performance is roughly equivalent to two 90-minute soccer games back-to-back or an 18-mile run.

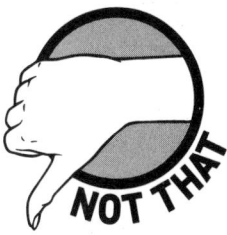

DATING

*T*he day is near when you'll want to spend some special time with a special someone you think is kind of special. *Ah, how embarrassing! Do we really need to talk about this?!* Actually, yes. Also known as dating, the act of spending time together to learn if you like them and if they like you is totally worth talking about. Now that you are middle school minded, think about this. What is dating? What isn't dating?

Let's start with what isn't. Acting silly to get attention isn't dating. That's called flirting. Staring from across the cafeteria isn't dating. That's called creepy. Going out of your way to walk by their locker between every class, following them home, and texting messages that took you an hour to thumb peck isn't dating. That's called stalking. Don't be a creepy stalker. Dating is when both of you agree that you are going to get to know each other better, slowly. Seriously, there is no need to rush into things socially, emotionally, or physically. Socially, you don't need to make a big announcement to all your friends, in person or online. Emotionally, if you are going to use the "L" word, choose "like" and not "love" till you are way past middle school. Physically, only go as far as you would if your parents were watching. This may all sound weird, and if it does don't worry, your future self will thank you.

True OR False?

Dates and figs are the same thing.

False. Figs and dates are two different types of fruits. Fig plants are shrubs, while dates are grown on trees.

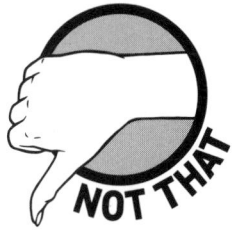

DESKS

*F*ront row or back corner? Beside the window for direct sun, or close to the door for a quick getaway? By yourself for better concentration, or by your friends for more conversations? There are so many choices for where you can sit in class, you might not be able to stand yourself! But before your head gets lost in the cloud of options, keep your feet on the ground and this in your mind. One teacher may give you free-range pickings for where to rest your rear, yet in your next class the teacher could assign your behind to a seating chart. One thing is certain—all desks are "public property." The class before you and the one following have other kids sitting in the same seat. So respect the desk and keep the row straight, circle curved, or group together. Always try to leave your desk as good as, if not better than, the way you found it.

 Quote

"On the first day of school, you got to be real careful where you sit. You walk into the classroom and just plunk your stuff down on any old desk, and the next thing you know the teacher is saying, 'I hope you all like where you're sitting, because these are your permanent seats.'"[7]

—Jeff Kinney, author of the Diary of a Wimpy Kid series

DETENTION

*I*t seems like everybody gets in trouble at school at least once. Trouble can range from something little, like forgetting to turn in homework and getting a bad grade on an assignment, to something serious that earns the discipline of detention. Google search the "meaning of detention," and the quick search results include the definition "the action of detaining someone . . . in official custody, especially as a political prisoner." Now STOP! Before you go and turn into a middle school student-rights activist, slow your roll and think for a minute. Consider that in the definition of the word *discipline* there is both the positive value of *knowledge* and negative action of *punishment*. Both are options. When you possess the positive value of self-discipline, you are more likely to do the right thing and not get disciplined with detention. Lack self-discipline, do the wrong thing, get in trouble, and be disciplined with detention. Basically you can have discipline and no detention or no discipline and get detention. The choice is yours. If you do find yourself *detained in official custody*, remember this wise advice from a seasoned 8th grader: Figure out what works, and do it as often as you can. Figure out what doesn't work, and stop doing it. That should keep you from getting in trouble more than once.

Pop Quiz

Q: What do ISS and OSS mean?

A: ISS stands for In-School Suspension. This means you stay at school, do some work around the school, and get your schoolwork done. OSS is Out-of-School Suspension. You can't come back to school till they say it's okay, and getting your schoolwork done is much more difficult without the help of teachers.

DRAMA

*H*ave you ever been in a situation where things got out of control really fast? All of a sudden something that wasn't that big of a deal becomes the biggest deal on the planet! Anytime a mountain is made out of a molehill, it's DRAMA. And I don't mean the kind of drama performed on a stage. Yet, it's called drama for a reason. We are all characters in our own story, and when exaggeration is injected and judgments get emotional, your story becomes a drama. WARNING! Exit stage left when excessive drama is detected. Usually the situation is full of half-truths and a few lies. Don't get pulled onstage for the tragedy. Stick to what is positive and keep in control of your thoughts, words, and actions. Life contains enough real drama of its own, so there is no need to produce more.

Looking Back

In middle school, being on stage with my friends in theater class was a lot of fun. Any drama that happened off the stage was never good. Being kind and supportive to each other was always the best of times!

—Erica Catherman

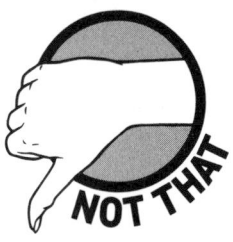

⊚⊚⊚⊚⊚⊚⊚⊚⊚⊚⊚ DRINKS ⊚⊚⊚⊚⊚⊚⊚⊚⊚⊚⊚

*T*hirsty much? Hope so, considering 60% of your body weight is water. Getting the wet stuff in is good for flushing out toxins from your body systems and carrying nutrients to your cells. Staying hydrated also helps keep your breath fresh and skin from getting too oily. A good goal is to drink about eight 8-ounce glasses of fluid a day. Everyone's body is dependent on fluids, yet few girls drink as much water as they need. Some even say they don't like the naturally tasteless flavor of water and prefer sipping down their fluids from an overpriced can of chemically sweetened carbonated water. Your preference for pure H_2O or H_2OCO_3 mixed with natural and artificial flavors is between you and your dentist. What you need to know about drinking water or soda at school is teachers, coaches, janitors, lunch assistants, bus drivers, and carpool parents all hate it when you spill. They're also not big fans of students leaving half-full drinks sitting around for somebody else to pick up or "accidentally" kick over. It's a good idea to check with your teacher/coach/driver about their beverage policy before you open a can of Get in Trouble at School.

Just Joking

What is the study of soda carbonation?

Fizzics

ELECTIVE CLASSES

Some classes you are required to take. Some classes you choose to take. Many of the core courses like math, language arts, science, and history are required learning. Elective classes like drama, robotics, band, and computer programming are open for your choosing. The trick is being proactive and thinking ahead while planning your school schedule to include both your required and elective classes. The good news is, most of the class scheduling process is decided for you each year. Yet within your schedule are one or two class openings where you can "Insert elective course here." But choose wisely, because once you have committed to an elective class, it can be difficult to near impossible to change your schedule. So, if Underwater Basket Weaving sounded cool when you signed up for it, but now Advanced Robotics is looking way better . . . it's probably too late. Don't forget to bring your scuba mask to class.

To Do in Middle School:

✓ Go on a class trip. Most grade levels plan a class trip at least once a year. It may be somewhere local, historical, or just for fun. Sometimes a class trip may even be an overnight adventure. Whatever the trip, be sure to get the most out of the opportunity. Have fun, learn some cool stuff, and try to make a new friend along the way.

EMOTIONS

*E*ver ridden a roller coaster? All those ups and downs, twists and turns, spins and death-defying drops can make a girl feel nervous, scared, and excited all at the same time. That's a lot like the emotional roller coaster known as middle school. One moment you're feeling up, and then down. One day it's "the best of your life" and the next "the worst ever!" Why so many emotional twists and turns? Because middle school is life's prime time for no two days to be the same socially, emotionally, or physically. This can push you toward feelings of excitement and terror all wrapped up in one. But don't worry, it's pretty normal and will eventually smooth out in a turn or two if you do your part to stay on track.

For instance, when your emotions drop, it's not a good time to fly off the rails and experiment with cursing your way through "expressing" yourself. Nobody likes a dirty mouth. Choose your descriptive words carefully and try to stick with "I" language like, "I feel frustrated right now." Stay away from the emotional whiplash that follows blaming others for how you feel, with statements like, "You are so frustrating!" They'll probably get defensive and say something back like, "No, I'm not. You are!" and there you go again—up and down, round and round on the vomit comet of emotional twists and turns. Instead, go for a smoother ride by sticking with "I" language and avoiding the roller-coaster run of "you" language. When your emotions do get crazy, and they will, take a minute to chill out and remember that you are in control of you. Take a few deep breaths, stay centered, and focus on the positive.

Pop Quiz

Q: Which is the best emoji face to use when breaking up with a "boyfriend" in a text message?

A: Trick question! Don't break up in a text message. Face-to-face is the way to go unless that's not an option.

FACE WASH

*L*et's just face the facts, ladies. Those zombie apocalypse webisodes you're addicted to watching will never actually happen, yet a real-life zit invasion is headed your way. Stop obsessing over fictitious herds of bad skin–covered corpses, and start planning how to defend your face from a puberty-planned pimple occupation. When it comes to fighting the effects of oily skin and acne, your best defense is a good offense. Start your day by washing your face in the shower. Wash again before going to bed each night. Always use a clean washcloth, mild face soap, and warm water.

How To . . .
Wash Your Face

STEP 1—Make it routine. Wash every day, morning and evening.

STEP 2—Wet a clean washcloth with warm water.

STEP 3—Hold the warm washcloth to your face and neck for a minute. This loosens dirt and opens your pores.

STEP 4—Apply the mild soap to your face and neck. A nonirritating and alcohol-free skin product works best. (You can buy this kind of skin cleanser at most grocery stores or pharmacies. Ask your parent or a store clerk for help picking one that will work for you.)

STEP 5—Rinse your skin. Use warm water.

STEP 6—Don't touch! Your hands are covered in bacteria, and bacteria love to make zits on your face.

STEP 7—Eat and drink better. Avoid greasy foods high in saturated fat, sugar, and salt. Drink lots of water.

FARTING

*A*s you know, girls pass gas just like boys do. There's no nice way to say it, so giving your backside outbursts cute names like *poof*, *toot*, or *fluffing* doesn't change the fact that you just farted. Basically, you are a walking science experiment that could blow up at any moment. Everywhere you go in school, a strange brew of noxious gasses ferments within you. Those bubbles building in your large intestine are produced "naturally" as your digestive system breaks down breakfast or lunch. The bloated feeling in your belly is nitrogen, hydrogen, carbon dioxide, and methane, which are all odorless gasses. If you are lucky, they might creep out undetected by the average nose. But mix in even a small amount of hydrogen sulfide or ammonia and your roux smells like . . . PEW! Was that you? Not if you pass on passing gas in class. Do the right thing and keep the air clean until you are outside. But when the pressure builds and you just can't hold it in any longer, please let it out in the bathroom.

Just Joking

If a queen farts, is it a noble gas?

(That joke was for you science lovers.)

FIGHTS

It's like some girls are looking for a fight. Maybe they are selfish bullies, angry at life, or their cell phone just fell in the toilet. Whatever the reason for their thin skin and rush to "fighting words," there is no need to meet them in a punching, slapping, hair-pulling brawl in the hall. Instead, show you are tough enough by being the girl in total control. Be quick to listen, slow to speak, slow to become angry, and the first to use your brain by turning and walking away. Instead of raising their fists, smart girls fight their battles with their brains. Not only is this a clever way to win, it also avoids the pain that comes with a potential bloody nose, bruised ego, and a suspension trip to the principal's office. Try to recall the wise words Queen Hippolyta shared with Princess Diana, also known as Wonder Woman, the next time you feel like clenching your fists: "Fighting doesn't make you a hero."[8] Unless you are in a boxing ring, the only fighting you should be doing is with the words you use to stand up for yourself and others who are unable to stand up for themselves. *That* is heroic.

Just Joking

Why don't skeletons fight each other?

They don't have the guts.

FIRE DRILLS

You know the drill. When wall-mounted sirens screech loud enough to make your ears want to bleed and mini strobe lights burn blue spots into your retina, it's a fire drill. The school is not actually about to burst into flame, yet . . . if a Bunsen burner had tipped over in science class and ignited the sweater you left dangerously close to an open flame, everybody would know how to get out of the building quickly and safely. But that's not the case today, so all you need to do is remember what you practiced back in the days of elementary school evacuations. Simply follow the teacher's instructions to make your way to the nearest fire-free zone. After a quick head count and the "all clear" is announced, you'll head back to class.

Do know that this is not the time to move slow, check your phone, or make a quick stop in the bathroom. Such behavior is not very bright and is guaranteed to make smoke blast out of your principal's ears while burning any chance you have of getting back on your science teacher's good side. Your best bet is to stay cool, calm, and cooperative through the entire drill. That and remember to move your sweater off the counter when you get back to class.

Pop Quiz

What three things are needed to make fire burn?
- (A) match, candle, paper
- (B) fuel, oxygen, heat
- (C) trees, marshmallow, tent

Answer: (B) fuel, oxygen, heat

⊚⊚⊚⊚⊚⊚⊚⊚⊚⊚ FOOD ⊚⊚⊚⊚⊚⊚⊚⊚⊚⊚

*H*ealth class teachers are guaranteed to say some funny stuff like, "You are what you eat, from your head down to your feet." Good thing this is not literally true. If such a statement were factual, some girls would look like a box of processed food parts soaked in an over-caffeinated carbonated beverage. Yet, what goes in must come out, and this happens in both obvious and obnoxious ways. The kind of food you eat and how much you stuff into your face has a direct effect on the quality of your life. The meals you choose power your daily energy levels, brain focus, the freshness of your breath, the smell of your gas, the size jeans you wear, and even the number of pimples present on your face. Basically, food is fuel. Do your best to eat fresh and healthy, avoid junk snacks, drink lots of water, and limit your allowance of processed foods you choose to chew.

To Do in Middle School:

✓ Volunteer at a food bank to support the work they are doing to supply food and grocery items to people in need.

FOOT ODOR

*O*kay, daydream about this for a minute. Imagine you are the first human to meet a tiny space alien whose ship crashed in your backyard. The extraterrestrial is peaceful and obviously really smart, because her head is huge (for a tiny alien). The little green girl likes you so much, our government makes you the alien's teacher about Earth's human stuff and a spy about space's alien stuff. All is good until your lessons about Earthlings include how our noses run and feet smell. In an attempt to help the confused alien understand the difference between runny noses and smelly feet, you offer the foreigner your shoe and a tissue. With only one sniff of your sneaker, the mini-Martian's skin turns from a light green to puke gray. She gasps for air, her nose implodes, and she chokes to death. To make a bad situation even worse, you learn the tiny alien is the royal daughter of the tiny alien queen with an even bigger head. This means you just killed the petite princess with your rank, stank toe jam. The alien queen believes you just assassinated her daughter. She declares war on the third rock from the sun and prepares to hyper jump her Dreadnought Warships into a battle with Earth. Who knew your foul foot funk could bring about the end of the world!

Well . . . just about every human being has smelled stinky feet and knows the feeling of total doom. So how can you fight off an imaginary alien invasion and avoid the real-life embarrassment of walking around school with smelly feet? Start with washing your feet with soap . . . EVERY DAY! Next, dry your toes before putting on clean socks. Finally, air out your shoes at the end of the day and buy a pair of odor-eating insoles if you need to. These simple actions can save both your reputation at school and the earth from total annihilation.

Strange but True

Did you know that each of your feet contains a whopping 250,000 sweat glands and can produce a full pint of sweat per day, per foot? That's a lot of shoe-dew.

◎◎◎◎◎◎◎◎ FRIENDS ◎◎◎◎◎◎◎◎◎

*E*verybody needs a few true friends. Some say the number of truly great friends a girl will have in her life can be counted on one hand. This is because there's a big difference between friends who will be there for you through thick and thin and virtual "friends" you collect after an attention-grabbing pic post. Your crew, squad, and sisters truly know you and you know them. The best of friends are the ones who make you laugh, inspire you to think about new things, challenge you to do cool stuff, and are always there to lift you up. They encourage you to succeed, and when you do, they won't take advantage of you or the situation. Choose your friends carefully, because you will be known by the ones you keep. This may mean you'll need to walk away from "friends" who are a bad influence. Most important, always be the kind of friend you'd like to befriend you.

 Quote

"Find a group of people who challenge and inspire you, and spend a lot of time with them, and it will change your life."[9]

—Amy Poehler

GAMING

*R*eality is for losers who don't play video games—unless you are playing in virtual reality, and then you won't believe how actual the graphics have become," says the gamer totally disconnected from reality. Don't be that girl. Sure, gaming can be a fun part of middle school and beyond. So is being a high-score holder in the reality game called life. Discovering the cheat codes to first-person interactions with family, teachers, friends, and other humanoids employs "reusable" hacks that work over and over again, just like in your favorite free roam or sandbox game. To keep your real-world FPS rate smooth, commit the time and attention needed to master the game of life just as you would with the latest and greatest digital download. For sure the realities awaiting you outside the game are just as challenging and way more immediate than your cred as a galaxy-protecting mutant mercenary.

True OR False?

The first video game was invented in 1971.

False. Physicist William Higinbotham created the first video game in October 1958. It was a very simple tennis game, similar to the classic 1970s video game Pong, and it was quite a hit at a Brookhaven National Laboratory open house.

GET TO CLASS ON TIME

Getting to class on time is not as difficult as you may think. To prove the point, consider the following challenge. Emma and Meg are in the same history class. The bell rings and they leave for their next class at the same time. Their goal is to Beat the Bell and get there in five minutes or less.

—Emma knows what she's doing. She first stops at her locker. Then she walks over to say hi to a friend. Next she makes a quick run to the bathroom, a stop at the trash can, and then straight to her next class. Total time 4:15.

—Meg chooses her own route. First, she goes to the bathroom, then to her locker. After stashing her history book in the locker, she heads outside into the courtyard to yell "hi" to her friends. She rushes back inside and wanders the full length of the hall and back again. She drops her backpack on the floor and tries to sneak up and surprise the new guy who she thinks is so cute. He sees her coming and heads the other way. Epic fail. Acting like it never happened, Meg forgets where she dropped her backpack and searches the hall to find it. She grabs her backpack and stops to get a drink of water just as the bell rings. Finally, she runs around the corner toward her next class. Total time 5:47. She's late . . . also known as tardy.

The moral of the story? To get to class on time—be an Emma, not a Meg.

Strange but True
Some teachers will count you tardy if you are not in class by the time the bell rings. Other teachers will count you tardy if you are not sitting in your desk by the time the bell rings. It's your responsibility to learn what each teacher means by "tardy."

SCHOOL MAP

SCHOOL MAP

GOSSIP

*T*he average human mouth can open wide enough to fit three fingers in between the upper and lower front teeth. That is, unless the words spilling from your mouth are gossip vomit, and then an entire foot may easily slip into the same space. "Foot in mouth" . . . what? It's just a saying, yet the meaning is time tested. You see, way back in the 1870s, foot-and-mouth disease was all the rage with cattle. This was a problem and usually meant the cow was foul. The expression "putting one's foot in one's mouth" began to be used as a metaphor for foul people who got in trouble for what they said. Sharing selfish secrets, half-truths, and hurtful gossiping got them in trouble then, just as it does today.

Here are a few rules you can use to avoid putting your foot in your mouth:

> **Rule #1**—If you have a problem with somebody, try talking *with* them rather than about them.
>
> **Rule # 2**—Ask yourself: Would you say to someone's face what you are wanting to say or post about them?
>
> **Rule # 3**—Talk about others the way you want them to talk about you.

If somebody is spreading gossipy stuff about you, refer back to Rule #1 and ask a trusted adult to go with you to talk with them.

 Quote

"Anyone who will gossip to you, will gossip about you."

—Anonymous

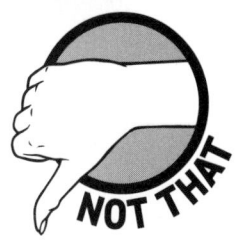

GRADES

*B*reaking news. Teachers don't "give" grades to students. Instead, students must "earn" their grades. Seriously, you've got to wrap your head around this one. In middle school you must do your part to pick up what the teacher is laying down. It doesn't matter whether or not you like the subject or teacher. Maybe you don't like the teacher's "style." Maybe you don't like the kids in your class. Do or don't, welcome to the big show. Middle school is all about you owning the effort you put into school to get the grades you need to succeed. For some girls, school comes easy. They still have to own their goal of getting straight A's in every class. Other girls will have a more difficult time in school. They too must do everything in their power to make a grade that passes them through their courses. Here are a few sure-to-work ways to start owning earning your grades:

1. Come to class, on time.
2. Listen to the teacher.
3. Get organized.
4. Take notes.
5. Ask questions.
6. Don't distract other students or the teacher.
7. Be kind to the teacher.
8. Be kind to the substitute teacher.
9. Do the work and TURN IT IN.
10. Do any and all extra-credit work.

How To . . .
Get Maximum Credit on Completed Classwork

STEP 1—Put your name on the top of the page.

STEP 2—Turn it in on time.

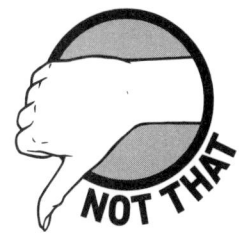

GRAMMAR

*N*ot long ago High English was the way people who wanted to sound smart talked. Slang-free and always proper, they spoke and wrote in a formal style that showed they knew the language of the educated class. Times have changed and so has the way people write and speak. In the world of a modern middle schooler, texting, messaging, and typing that is automatically spell-checked, auto filled, and abbreviated is perfectly normal. Similarly, the way some people speak has come to include verbal fuzz, mumbling, abbreviations, and slang that may or may not be understood by a teacher, coach, parent, and other students. Said simply, poor grammar can lead to a wealth of confusion. Avoid the confusion and show people just how smart you are by practicing two simple rules of good grammar.

Rule #1—Speak up. You have a wonderful voice, so speak with the clear confidence people need to hear and understand you.

Rule #2—Write well. Teachers don't accept text message abbreviations in sentences, so spell out every word, using every letter.

When you speak and write well, people are more likely to understand, recognize, and respect you as a member of today's educated class.

Pop Quiz

1. What is the shortest sentence in the English language?

2. More English words begin with this letter than any other letter of the alphabet.

3. What is the longest English word that can be spelled without repeating any letters?

Answers: 1. "I am." 2. The letter *s* 3. uncopyrightable

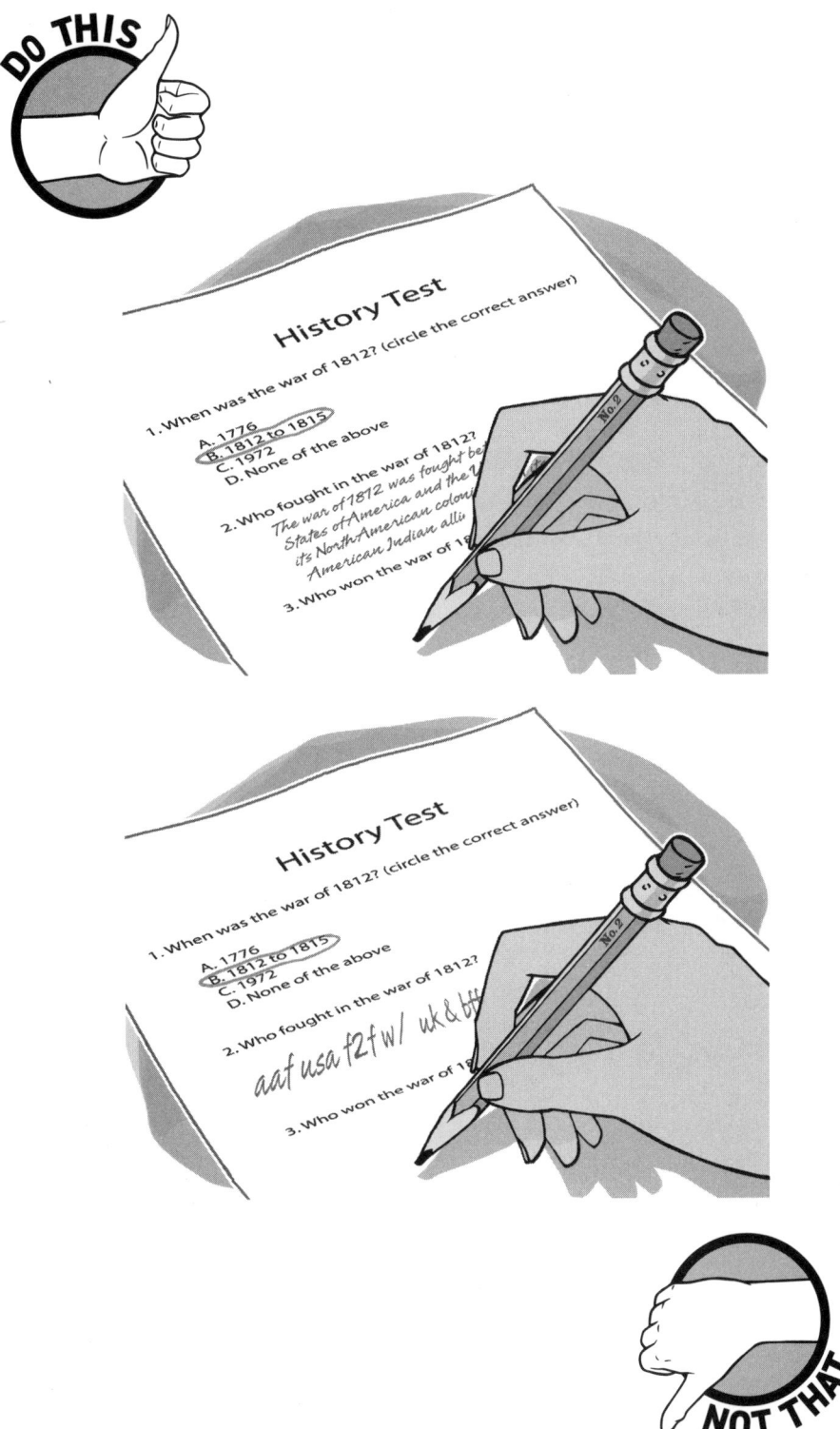

GUY FRIENDS

*G*irls are friends with their girl friends in very different ways than guys are friends with their guy friends. Girls create friend titles like "besties" and "BFF" while posting pictures of their hands held together in the shape of a shared heart. Um, most guys don't do that. Girls will text their bestie nonstop while sitting right next to each other. Yeah, most guys don't do that either. What a girl shares with her girl friends includes, well, pretty much everything—clothes, makeup, headphones, and secrets, in ways most guys don't easily understand. Here's an example. Some girls will say to a guy, "You can tell me. I won't tell anybody." Now, when a girl says "anybody," that doesn't necessarily mean a BFF won't find out. This is because BFFs aren't just "anybody." A best friend forever is such a close friend, it's like the two are one person. Yet this kind of close poses a problem for many guys. They don't share everything with their guy friends. Two guys can be both good friends and still not tell each other everything.

To keep it simple, don't expect your guy friends to act much different with you. They are probably not going to tell you everything either. That and don't expect them to be as complimentary as your girl friends. Understand it or not, now you know.

Strange but True

BFF is the airport code for Western Nebraska Regional airport, as well as an abbreviation for an Australian Bush Fire Fighter and the British Fighting Force.

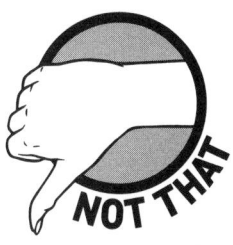

HAIR

*M*iddle school is filled with unexpected challenges and more than a few frustrations. Finding a hairstyle that works shouldn't add stress to your life. Yet for some girls it does. Either they don't care that their head looks like a dirty mop, or they spend more time than Miss America directing each and every follicle into hair-spray-sculpted perfection. You don't need to be either of those girls. Instead, work your style until you find a 'do that works for you. Don't be afraid to try a few different looks before deciding on what works best for you and your hair. Next, find a stylist who knows how to cut your hair the way you like, and stick with them. After that, use good hair products to keep your style looking right. And please, for the sake of the noses surrounding you in class, never, never, ever apply fragrance-scented hair gels, paste, sprays, or other trendy smelling goo to your 'do.

Strange but True

Hair is strong. A single strand could hold 100 grams or 3 ounces in weight, but combined, the hair of a whole head could support 12 tons, or the weight of two elephants.[10]

⊚⊚⊚⊚⊚⊚⊚⊚⊚⊚ **HALL PASS** ⊚⊚⊚⊚⊚⊚⊚⊚⊚⊚

*T*o travel freely over borders and between countries in the world requires you to carry a valid passport. To freely move around the school when you should be in class requires an official hall pass. Those are guarded like government-issued official travel documents. Most teachers don't just hand them out to anybody who asks. You'll need to pass two hall-pass application requirements. First, do you really need to go from here to there? Getting called out of class to visit the office, advisor, or media center, or to deliver something from one teacher to another is approved hall-pass travel. "Needing" to get another drink of water, check your locker, or faking a request to see the school nurse just as the math test starts are all unapproved travel requests and will be denied. Second, do you respect the power of the pass? Your reputation for past hall-pass behavior can make or break your future pass privileges. The hall pass permits you the privilege to quickly go from point A to point B and back again. Hall passes are not a get-out-of-class pass, releasing you to free-range wander around the school. Respect the pass and all it permits you.

Ask a Middle School Survivor

Q: When can I get a hall pass?

A: Hall passes are privileges. Getting a pass to try and hang out with your friends isn't a good idea. They should be used to go to the bathroom or get some water. If you abuse the privilege you won't get a pass again.

Anna B., from North Carolina

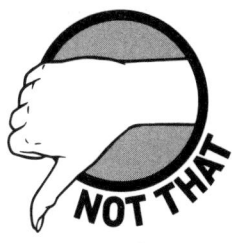

HALLWAYS

*H*allways are the highways of school. Routes exist to move the middle school masses and their cargo from one school stop to the next. Like downtown traffic during rush hour, your school hallways will occasionally get all jammed up bumper-to-bumper and even report a few shoe flat-tires and fender-bender backpack accidents. To keep traffic moving and the hall cops off your tail, follow these basic road rules to arrive at your next destination on time. Always walk on the right side, yield to 8th graders, look both ways when turning toward the lockers—and no parking in the middle of the hall! People stop being polite when a "few friends" stand in the middle of the flow "just talking." Like a dam they back everything up, and frustrations grow deep, fast. When they do break free, it's a slow rush to beat the bell through the very mess they created.

How To . . .
Pick Up Your Papers When Dropped in the Hallway

STEP 1—Stop, drop, and protect your papers. They are about to get trampled. Don't just stand there and look confused.

STEP 2—Scoop up the dropped papers. Don't worry about keeping them in order.

STEP 3—Stand back up and keep moving. Hold on to your papers tight so you don't drop them again.

STEP 4—Step aside and try to organize the mess of papers you hold. If something is missing, go back and attempt a recovery mission.

HAND WASHING

*T*hink about all the stuff you touch at school. Your two hands grip doorknobs, handrails, seats, lockers, desks, hall walls, gym floors, and countless other sticky surfaces. Then with filthy fingers you dig around in your bag for a sharp pencil. One minute later you stick that putrid pencil in your mouth. Without thinking about it, you just chewed on a yellow #2 stick of germs, bacteria, and microscopic viruses. One way to combat self-contamination is to wash your hands a few times a day at school. For sure wash them after every visit to the bathroom, before lunch, and after science class, gym class, and trips through the locker room. Wash for at least 20 seconds (enough time to sing the "Happy Birthday" song twice). Think you can handle it?

Strange but True

"A large percentage of foodborne disease outbreaks are spread by contaminated hands. Appropriate hand washing practices can reduce the risk of foodborne illness and other infections."[11]

—Centers for Disease Control and Prevention

⊚⊚⊚⊚⊚⊚⊚ HANDWRITING ⊚⊚⊚⊚⊚⊚⊚

*T*he ancient Egyptians wrote in hard-to-read scripts called *hieroglyphs.* To read and understand their writings requires the keen eye of a trained professional. Well, you're not Cleopatra, and your mummy may still need to help you with your English homework, so leave the archaeologists in the sand and let's work on your handwriting. For the last six years you have practiced your writing skills, which means you should be pretty good at it by now. Capitalizing letters at the beginning of each sentence, crossing your t's, dotting your i's, and fitting each word between the lines on the paper is exactly what teachers expect of all middle school students. If you still insist on wandering all over the page with your words, scratching out letters that you don't even recognize, and ending sentences with odd punctuation marks that include a heart-shaped dot, then move to the desert and chisel your hieroglyphs into the walls of a pyramid. No? Well then, slow your scroll, keep it between the lines, and always remember your penmanship.

Just Joking

What did the paper say to the pencil?

Write on.

HOME ROOM

*I*t's been said that a girl's home is her castle. You know who lives in castles? Queens. You know who lives in the castle's dark and dirty dungeon? Lazy jokers. Don't be the lazy joker who claims it's regal to carpet her room with dirty clothes, molding food, and "lost" homework. Instead, be the ruler of your kingdom and govern your room with a decree to keep the space clean enough for a royal.

Strange but True

Having a clean room or space has been linked to self-control and making better choices in regards to food and delaying gratification for a better outcome. Messy rooms or spaces have been linked to creativity . . . and higher allergies and illness due to higher levels of dust, dead skin cells, molds, and bacteria.[12]

HOMEROOM

*T*he plan for homeroom is to start the school day off right. Often home-room time is used for teachers to take attendance, share some announcements, and get ready for the day ahead. Yet some girls feel their homeroom at school is an extension of their room at home. These girls figure if they were home, they would be sleeping, so why not catch some z's at school too? Well, rise and shine, ladies! Think of the school bell that starts homeroom as your second alarm clock, without the snooze option. The sun is up, you are awake, and the school day is ready to go.

To Do in Middle School:

✓ Join a club or sport.

HOMEWORK

Some teachers are all about assigning homework and some are not. Some class subjects require you to read, study, write, or prepare outside of assigned time in school. There is no predicting how often or how much homework middle school will require, but one thing is for certain—it's best to get it done and handed in . . . on time. The crazy but true part is that teachers often see girls "forget" to hand in finished homework more often than they actually forget to finish their homework. That's like going out to dinner, ordering, and paying for the food . . . but forgetting to eat it. Once you get it done, hand it in . . . on time. Oh, and one more thing. Make sure to put your name on your homework before you get it done and handed in . . . on time.

Just Joking

What did the calculator say to the math student?

You can count on me.

LEADERSHIP

*D*o you want to be a leader? Good. You will need to be more influential than you are easily influenced. If you are influential, then you can be a leader. An easy-to-remember definition of leadership is *Leadership is influence, used for good.* Middle school is the prime time to dream, discover, and develop your levels of influence to benefit both yourself and others. First, you'll need to practice self-leadership. Begin with taking responsibility for your own actions and doing what's right, even when nobody is watching. Work hard to get better at what you enjoy and practice the life skills and moral character that will help you move from where you are to where you need to go. Add in some time management skills and you'll be the leader of you. Second, look for opportunities to lead others. Leading others requires you to treat them as you would want to be treated, listen well, and value teamwork. When others see these values in you, they will want to follow and learn from you. That's when it happens. By using your influence for good, you'll have become a leader.

Quote

"Do not wait for leaders; do it alone, person to person. Be faithful in small things because it is in them that your strength lies."

—Mother Teresa

LOCKDOWNS

*A*s you know, every school must perform lockdown drills. "Lockdown. Lockdown. Lockdown." Not much has changed since you practiced lockdowns in elementary school, so you know what to do and what not to do. There is no need to make it into something it's not or to draw attention to yourself. Instead, do the right thing and keep calm, follow instructions, stay hidden, remain still, be quiet, and don't mess around. The school receives a grade on how well the drill goes, and the higher the grade, the better.

Ask a Middle School Survivor

Q: Are lockdowns the same in middle school as they were in elementary?

A: Really, lockdowns are the same in all schools. If you have experienced a lockdown in elementary school, it's the same in middle and high school. The rules are all the same. Nobody gets in the building and nobody gets out.

Brenda L., from Florida

LOCKER LOCKS

*M*iddle school may be your first experience with lockers. Love them or not, lockers provide a safe place to store your things so you don't have to carry around extra stuff from class to class. Remembering to lock your locker is a really good idea. Forgetting how to unlock your locker is a really bad feeling.

Mind-blanking your locker combination is often followed by a feeling of panic and an audible "AAAAHHHHHHHH!" What if you can't get your book for next period, or even worse . . . your lip gloss! In an effort to avoid such a tragic moment, follow this two-step procedure:

> *Step 1*—Memorize your locker combination and practice cracking the code as many times as you need to never forget it. Seriously, drill those numbers so deep into your brain you'll still remember them the day you graduate from high school.

> *Step 2*—Repeat step 1 until you get it right, every time.

How To . . .
Open a Standard Combination Lock

> *Turn #1*—Spin right (clockwise) three full turns. Stop at your FIRST number.

> *Turn #2*—Spin left (counterclockwise) one full turn, passing the FIRST number, and stop at the SECOND number.

> *Turn #3*—Spin right (clockwise) and stop at the THIRD number.

Pull open lock.

LOCKER ROOMS

*H*opefully, the locker room swamps are a thing of the past. No longer forced to shower in front of others, we now use the locker room as a place to quickly change before and after gym. Not that girls sweat (we glisten) . . . but maybe a little perspiration made its way onto your gym clothes, making it a good idea to change into something fresh. Although showers are out, making sure you have a clean shirt to change into and a fresh swab of deodorant is a good idea. No need to let bacteria start growing on your glistening perspiration. Take care to keep your bag and clothes off the floor as it's a petri dish of germs, mold, and fungus down there. For the same reason, you need to stay off the tiles too. Sit on the benches and chairs, or stand if you must. Just stay up off the floor! Also, just like you do following a visit to the bathroom, always wash your hands after using the locker room. Though you don't take showers at school, make sure that you get one at home. Consider hygiene your homework and shower each and every day . . . it keeps the stinky bacteria away!

Ask a Middle School Survivor

Q: Is it weird to change clothes in a locker room with other girls around?

A: Changing with other girls in a locker room isn't as bad as it seems. Everyone is doing the same thing. You get in, change, and get out. It's really no big deal.

Greta M., from Oregon

LOCKERS ⊚⊚⊚⊚⊚⊚⊚⊚⊚⊚

Girls are known to love their lockers. Some decorate, theme, and create a DIY space worth showing off. However, over the course of a school year that neat space can start to slide into the gutter with snack wrappers, dirty gym shirts, trash paper, and a few "missing" items building up in the bottom of the space. Basically, if you need to call in a search party to locate a library book in your locker's rubble, you've got a problem. But you can avoid the slide by keeping your locker nice and neat. Maintain love for your locker by keeping it free of trash, unneeded papers, and for sure those smelly gym clothes—take them home and wash them. This will keep your locker shining all year long. Pictures and flashing string lights are optional!

Ask a Middle School Survivor

Q: How many times a day will I get to go to my locker?

A: It depends on your school and the rules they have. If you have "free" passing time, meaning you can go where you want during your passing time before your next class, then you can go to your locker when you want. Sometimes, instead of going to your locker after/before every class, it helps to bring stuff for two or three classes so you don't have to go to your locker so much.

Emily R., from Iowa

LOST AND FOUND

So you have cleaned out your locker but still have an item missing. Chances are good it's been collected and is now in the middle school lost and found—a great place to find "lost" items you didn't mean to leave behind in class, gym, or on the bus. It's pretty funny to see what items go missing. Here's a short list of real items lost and found in middle school.

Found

cowboy hat, straw	eyeglasses, prescription
jacket, size M	birthday card, Sarah's 12th
lunch bag	hammock
mini Statue of Liberty	beach ball, multicolor
math binder, algebra	retainer case, with retainer
snow pants, blue	dog collar, no dog
fishing pole, no line	plastic globe, coin inside
black glove, left hand	flashlight, no batteries
headphones, red	tree ornament, Christmas
diary, unlocked	tablet, green case
backpack, green	shoe, right

"Found—shoe, right" . . . Really?! Who loses one of two shoes and doesn't notice? How did that girl walk home from school, thinking, "Something feels different. I don't know exactly what, just different." Really? Look down. You're missing a shoe! If you find yourself claiming the title of The One-Shoed Wonder or just can't find your jacket, lunch bag, glove, or mini Statue of Liberty, take the time to stop by the school's lost and found. You may have to dig through the collection of unclaimed treasures for your missing jewel. Just remember, finders keepers only applies if it really is yours. There's no "shopping" for five-finger discounts in the lost and found.

Just Joking

What do you call a bear that lost its teeth?

A Gummie Bear

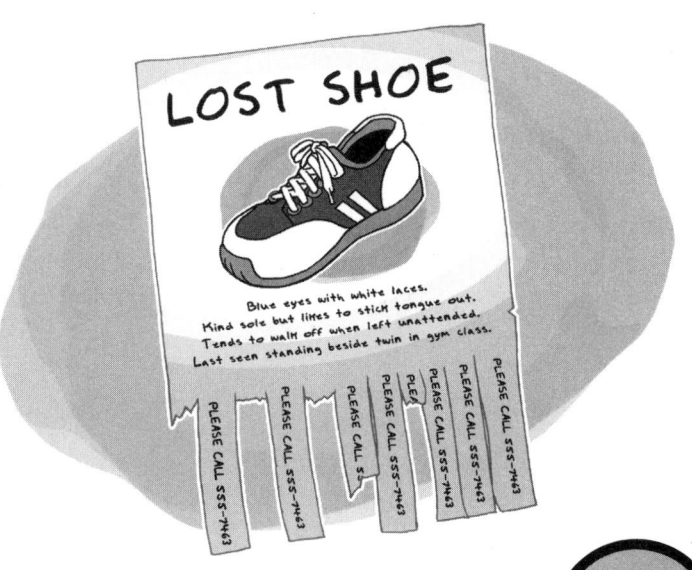

LUNCH

*E*veryone's heard an adult say, "Don't talk with your mouth full. It's rude." If you can't remember ever hearing such table instructions, you were polite from birth or you forgot—again. Lunchtime is a balance between talking with your friends and eating your food. Your body needs the fuel while your friends need to talk about the latest episode of your favorite show or YouTube video. The good news is you can do both, just not at the same time. The rule is simple. Say it, don't spray it. Eat a few bites. Chew and swallow. Talk for a minute. Take a drink. Swallow. Take another bite. While chewing with your mouth closed, be a good listener to what your friends are saying. Swallow. Talk again. Repeat. Lunch is also a good time to work on making new friends. Try a new table, be inclusive, ask someone who is sitting alone to join your table. Who knows, you could make a new friend or make someone's day!

True OR False?

Eating with your mouth open is considered polite in some cultures.

True. In some cultures, slurping while drinking and chewing with your mouth open shows the cook or host that you find the food delicious, while in other cultures such behavior would be considered extremely offensive. So be sure to study up before you chow down.

LUNCH LINE

"*N*ext in line. Next in line, please. What do you want for lunch today, sweetie? Fruit with that? A cookie too? How about some milk or juice with your meal? Next in line, please. Next in line."

Making your way through the school lunch line is a lot like selecting a meal at your local fast-food restaurant. True, there are fewer choices, no soda, and you can't mega-size a school lunch—but you're still supposed to move fast through the food line. Just like ordering at McJacks or Taco King, it's best to know your options before it's your turn. Waiting to decide until after the lunch person is staring at you is too late. Make your choice, fill your tray, and don't forget a drink. Finally, don't rush, and no pushing as you head into the lunchroom to find your friends.

How To . . .
Pack Your Own Lunch

STEP 1—Select leftovers from the refrigerator or make a fresh sandwich.

STEP 2—Pick a healthy balance of food that includes a main item, fruit or vegetable, and a treat. Don't forget a bottle of water.

STEP 3—Put each food item into a sealed plastic bag or approved food container.

STEP 4—Pack all your lunch items in a lunch bag or box. Add an ice pack if you've got perishables, like meat or dairy or mayo.

*G*ood thing the childish taunt "Liar, liar, pants on fire" is far from factual. If it were a statement of the obvious, how often would smoke trail up from behind you following a fib? One thing is for certain: When you lie, you're going to get burned. Teachers, principals, coaches, and even bus drivers are really good at turning up the heat when they know your story lacks honesty. Chances are they have heard the same tall tale told before and recognize your false testimony for what it really is. A lie. So, face the facts and be truthful. Honestly, it's much cooler.

Just Joking

Never trust the periodic table.

It makes up everything.

MEAN GIRLS

*M*ean girls are like skunks. From far off, they can be avoided. But when one crosses your path, life can really start to stink. So follow your nose and steer clear of the haters. That's all a mean girl really is—a hater. For some very real reason, they don't like themselves much and are choosing to take their frustrations out on others. Don't be that girl. Instead, be kind to everybody. Even the mean girl haters? Yes, even them. But when you do find yourself on the stink end of a mean girl's day, don't freak out and draw attention to yourself. Instead, try to stick with your friends and go immediately to talk with an adult you trust—like a teacher, advisor, or school administrator.

If *you* make fun of other people to make yourself feel better, that is mean. Mean is weak and hurtful. It doesn't matter if you think it's funny, teasing, or sarcasm. If it's tearing someone else down, that is mean and weak and stinks.

> "You can tell who the strong women are. They are the ones building each other up rather than tearing each other down."
>
> —Anonymous

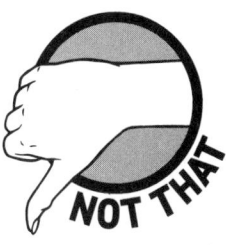

⟨⟨⟨⟨ MEDIA CENTER/LIBRARY ⟨⟨⟨⟨

See those rectangular things on the shelf? Those are called books. They are like TV for smart people. The media center has them stacked all over the place. Those machines on the tables are computers. Like books, they too can open doors to discovery, lead to great adventures, and be your ticket to more information than any one person could consume in their lifetime. Or, the media center may seem like slow, quiet torture for the middle school student who thinks they already know all they need to succeed. Why read when there's a video? Why study when Google knows all the answers? Why, why, why? Well, because only a fool hates wisdom and learning. And you're no fool. So, enjoy a little quiet time. Crack the cover of a book and use a computer for more than videos. You never know what you'll discover.

To Do in Middle School:

✓ Find and visit with a couple of your favorite teachers from grades past. Thank them for all they taught you and share your current successes with them.

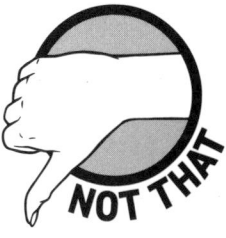

MONEY

*M*oney is like magic. With a simple distraction and sleight of hand, it can disappear into thin air. Now you see it. *Poof!* Now you don't. And what do you have left? An empty soda can, a crumpled bag, and a bad case of what feels like indigestion but is really buyer's remorse from getting what you didn't need and now don't want. The trick to managing money in middle school is figuring out how cash works more like a tool and less like candy. "Yeah, but I like candy," is what you're thinking—and you're right, who doesn't?

The truth is, the older you get, the bigger and more expensive the things you buy get. So now is the time to master your money and stop believing the illusion that your money grows as you do. The truth is, you are running out of teeth to put under your pillow, the few bucks your grandparents slip into a birthday card only comes around once a year, and your parents are not an open bank vault. What money you can make from pet sitting, babysitting, or doing extra work around the house can be put to work for you. Here's how. Save in the bank as much as you can, spend as little as you must, and give to charity as if you were the one in need. This makes you the master of your money and keeps you from being mastered by money's many sweet illusions.

"Winning with money is simple, live on less than you make."[13]

—Rachel Cruze

NAIL TRIMMING

*A*ccording to the Guinness World Records, the woman with the longest fingernails ever was an American named Lee Redmond.[14] The combined length of her 10 fingernails was over 28 feet, 4 inches. That's an average of over 14 feet per hand or 34 inches per finger. Not so great for putting on makeup, but you can bet she could scratch every inch of her back. Don't be the long-nailed version of Lee at your school. Keep your fingernails trimmed and whatever you do, NO biting! Want some glam hands? Read "How to Trim Your Fingernails" and "How to Apply Nail Polish" in our book *The Girls' Guide to Conquering Life.*

Strange but True

Lots of germs and some nasty bacteria live under your fingernails. What kind, you ask? The kind that hang on after making a trip to the bathroom, touching your shoes, or petting a dog. Think about that fun fact next time you nibble on your nails.

NAME ON YOUR PAPER

*Y*ou did all that homework. You studied, researched, and worked hard to write an A-grade paper. You stuffed it into your backpack, went to school, and even remembered to turn it in on time. A few days later the teacher hands back the graded assignments and yours is "missing." She points you to a stack of papers on her desk, and there you discover your work. Graded down from a B+ to C+. What the what? Then you see it. Across the top of the page is written, "No name." What! You forgot to put your name on the top of the page. Seriously? After all that hard work, you forgot the simplest part of the assignment? The only part you are guaranteed to get right? Come on, girl! Name it and claim it. Always remember to put your name on the paper before handing it in.

How To . . .
Remember Somebody's Name

STEP 1—Introduce yourself. Tell them your name and ask theirs.

STEP 2—Repeat their name in your head and in a sentence. Like this. "You said your name is Shawn? Nice to meet you, Shawn."

STEP 3—Try to associate them with somebody else you know with the same name.

STEP 4—Use their name whenever you talk with them. This will burn their name into your memory.

⊙⊚⊙⊚⊙⊚⊙⊚⊙⊚⊙⊚ ONLINE ⊙⊚⊙⊚⊙⊚⊙⊚⊙⊚⊙⊚⊙⊚

*B*ut I found it on the internet, so it has to be true." Um . . . no. Just because you read something online does not make it true. The truth is, back in 1983, researchers began assembling a computer-based "network of networks" to share data between universities and government organizations around the globe. This early version of what would become the internet wasn't very cool until 1990 when a British computer scientist named Tim Berners-Lee, also known as TimBL, invented the World Wide Web. From then to now, the interweb has spun from telephone landline dial-up to wireless go-anywhere connectivity. People used to "go online" occasionally. Today you live much of your life online. From googling "who is TimBL" to the GPS location tracker on your phone, you are leaving digital footprints, fingerprints, and imprints everywhere you virtually and actually go. This can make your life easier or bring it crashing back to reality. Keep your posts pure and you'll be cool with your teachers, parents, future college applications, and job interviews. Remember, it's important that you never share personal information about yourself online! Go rogue while connected and you'll have some explaining to do about what your eyes have seen, thumbs have clicked, and where you were online when that spyware accidentally infected your device.

Strange but True

The first website went live way back in 1991. It is dedicated to information about the World Wide Web and is still active today. You can check it out for yourself at http://info.cern.ch/hypertext /WWW/TheProject.html.

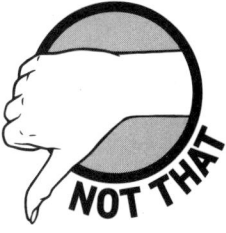

PARENTS

*C*hances are when your parents were in middle school, there were no seat belt laws, bike helmets, bottled water, smartphones, or social media, and online cat videos weren't a thing. Their idea of password protection was a secret phrase whispered in a friend's ear before entering a tree fort or cushion castle. A lot has changed since your parents were in middle school, so you'll have to give them a break every now and then when they just don't understand. Really, parenting is no easy task. Few other adventures in life can bring more joy or pain to a person than the responsibility and privilege of parenting. You'll want to add to the privilege they have of raising you by scoring some positive points with the parental units as often as possible. Here are two of the best ways: Spend time with them and talk to them. Time spent together and talking about stuff, or through stuff, is how good relationships are built. The better your relationship, the happier both you and your parents will be. They may not know what it's like to be in middle school today, but you can teach them. They may or may not agree with all you share, but you'll be amazed how smart they become by the time you're a parent and your kids are in middle school.

 Quote

"A father's goodness is higher than the mountain, a mother's goodness deeper than the sea."

—Japanese Proverb

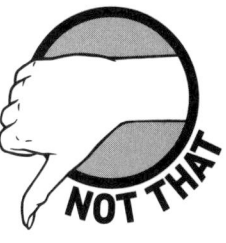

PDA

It's only appropriate to get technical here. PDA is the abbreviation for *Public Display of Affection*. No duh, right? But have you ever really thought about how odd middle school PDA can be?

Public: (adjective) open to all persons

Display: (verb) to show or exhibit; make visible; flaunt

Affection: (noun) fond attachment, devotion, or love

Basically, PDA is putting the physical side of a "relationship" on show for all to see. There are varying degrees of PDA. On the body contact Richter scale, "0" equals nobody ever sees you two together and "10" equals everybody knows everything. A PDA hug registers in at about "2." We're not even going to discuss holding hands, kissing, or other stuff, as most schools discourage that kind of physical affection anywhere on campus. And that's probably a good thing when we consider most relationships in middle school don't last very long. Like only a couple of days to a few weeks "not long." Just because you are "going out" doesn't mean you need to be "making out" in the hall. Nobody wants, or needs, to see that. Dealing with math tests and forgotten locker combinations is tough enough.

Did You Know?

There's no such thing as "butterfly kisses." As kids we received fluttered eyelash "kisses" against our cheeks and were told they were butterfly kisses. The truth is, butterflies do not have any lips or teeth, just a long, coiled tongue. Gross.

PERFUME

*T*he world's first recorded chemist was a perfume maker named Tapputi. Her methods for distilling flowers, oils, calamus, cyperus, myrrh, and balsam date back to 1200 BC. But Tapputi's infusions were not the first fragrances to float through the air. Early mixologists throughout the Mediterranean, Mesopotamia, India, and Asia all experimented with fragrant scents to both sweeten the air and mask the foul smells. What we wear today and call *perfume* is named such from a Latin word that literally means "through smoke." Apply it properly in small amounts. Never are you to splash or spray a smoldering, thick *through smoke* cloud of the perfume on yourself, your clothes, or anybody else. The perfume you choose was not mixed to mask your BO, advertise your arrival, or loiter in the air long after you walk by. Wear it sparingly, and only occasionally, if you wear it at all.

How To . . .
Apply Perfume

STEP 1—Pick one scent. Don't mix scented body wash, deodorant, and hair products in the same air as your perfume.

STEP 2—Remove cap. Point away from your eyes when doing so.

STEP 3—Apply perfume. Spray or dab a light amount to the skin on the base of your neck, wrist, or even behind the knee. Never apply to fabric, as the smell will change and stains can occur.

STEP 4—Recap perfume. You don't want to deal with a spill.

PHYSICAL EDUCATION

*S*ome girls look forward to PE class as a welcome break from the rear-numbing task of holding down a desk chair. Other girls walk to gym class thinking, "I'm really more of the brainiac type." Well, guess what? Like it or not, exercise boosts the brain's power. Girls who move more than their mouth outperform seat surfers in simple tasks like long-term memory, reasoning, attention, and problem solving.[15] It's true, look it up. That, and a healthy young woman like yourself is capable of walking about 12 miles a day without feeling the pain. Unless you haven't moved that far in weeks, which means you're probably growing tired from just holding this book. Look at it this way. Physical education class is way more than running, jumping, and doing sports-like stuff a few times a week. Exercising your body builds your muscle strength, physical coordination, and brain-processing power. Put all those benefits together, and it's good to know that if the zombie apocalypse ever does come, you'll be able to both outthink and outrun the walking dead.

Ask a Middle School Survivor

Q: What should I know about changing from gym clothes back into my school clothes?

A: Changing shorts and a T-shirt is no big deal. Just remember to take your gym clothes home each day to wash them and ALWAYS have deodorant to apply during the school day.

Caroline L., from Alabama

☙☙☙☙☙☙☙☙ POP QUIZZES ☙☙☙☙☙☙☙☙

*O*kay, everybody. Please put your books away, sharpen a pencil, and prepare to take an unscheduled test.

Question #1—What is the secret to passing pop quizzes in middle school?

"No, no, don't tell me. I know this one."

The answer is _____ *(Fill in the blank)*

Or would you prefer to try your luck with multiple-choice answers?

(A) I studied for this all week.

(B) I looked at the chapter practice questions last night for three minutes.

(C) I cheat off the answers of the kid sitting next to me.

(D) All of the above.

Answer: (A) There is no need to question the fact that middle school is a virtual minefield of both expected and surprisingly too-frequent "I didn't know we had a quiz today!" tests. From the weekly exam to pop quizzes that come out of nowhere, the only answer to passing tests in class and life is to study ahead and be prepared for the unexpected. Good luck.

Correction . . . good studying.

Just Joking
What kind of tree does a math teacher climb?

Geometry

⊚⊚⊚⊚⊚ PREPARED FOR CLASS ⊚⊚⊚⊚⊚

*Y*ou beat the bell and made it to class on time. Now, are you prepared for class to start? Ask any teacher and they will agree the top 10 things you need to bring to class each day include the following:

1. Pencil (with eraser)
2. Pen (blue or black)
3. Lined paper (wide or college ruled, depending on the class)
4. Completed homework (finished before class starts)
5. Class textbook (when provided)
6. School-provided technology (charged and ready to go)
7. Calculator (a must for math and science)
8. Personal technology (if allowed)
9. Rested eyes (that means sleeping in your bed, at night, and not in class)
10. Self-motivation, confidence, drive, grit, humility, manners, and a willingness to learn (okay, that's seven unique traits, but just saying "character" wouldn't do)

True OR False?

It's the teacher's job to hand out pencils to whoever forgot one.

False

PRINCIPAL

Who's the boss? You know, the big shot, big cheese, big wig, big kahuna? Kingpin, kingfish, King Kong? Top dog, top brass, guru, all pro, CEO? Who's the brains around here? The principal is, of course. But why? What have they done to deserve the leader of leaders title? Well, most public school principals have earned at least a master's if not a doctoral degree. That means they were in school as a student for somewhere between 17 and 19 years before getting the job. That doesn't even count the years of experience they had in the classroom as a teacher or in the front office as a vice principal. It's a pretty good bet that they've been around school longer than you've been alive. It's also pretty safe to say they chose to work in middle school because they like you. "But, what's not to like?" you ask. Really? Middle school administration is not the easiest way to make a living. Your principal has to deal with a limitless flow of drama, crazy hormones, and know-it-alls, and a daily dose of "What just happened here?" To make both your day and theirs the best it can be, try introducing yourself to the principal. Let them know you appreciate them and all they do for the school. Sound strange? Come on, this is middle school. You can do it. And don't worry. The principal may be the top dog around campus, but they don't bite.

True OR False?

Some principals are so committed to their job they sleep at the school.

True. A principal in Asotin, Washington, told his students that if they could raise $10,000 in the school fundraiser he would sleep on the school roof overnight. Students raised $22,000 in pledges, and Principal Nicholas slept on the roof, in a tent, in a sleeping bag, in the middle of October.[16]

PROBLEM SOLVING

*O*ne of the biggest differences between immature and mature middle school students is their ability to problem solve. Immature students need their teachers, parents, and friends to solve all their problems. Mature students work to resolve their problems on their own the best way they know how. Immature people say stuff like, "I can't do the work because I don't have a pencil." Mature problem solvers ask a friend for a pencil before the test begins. When two students fight over who gets to sit by the window during a science lab, they are immature. When they work together to move two chairs together on the window side of the lab table, they are mature. If "You didn't tell me what homework I missed when I was absent" has ever crossed your lips and assaulted a teacher's ears . . . yep, you guessed it. Immature. By asking the teacher, "I missed class yesterday and am wondering what homework was assigned," you demonstrate your maturity level and ability to problem solve.

True Story

The movie *Hidden Figures* is based on the true story of the problem-solving women of NASA's "human computers" who made it possible to send Americans into space. The film celebrates the African-American women who worked as unsung heroes personally computing the complex equations needed to send an astronaut into space and return them home again safe. Like you, these ladies had to show their work as they crunched the numbers to prove the math. The significance of their calculations added up to mission success in 1962 when astronaut John Glenn successfully orbited the globe three times.

PUBERTY

*A*s much as your school life is changing, so is your body. Thanks to puberty, a daily shower is a must. Soon your hair will grow out of your legs, underarms, and in places you guard like PRIVATE PROPERTY. Your chest will mature, zits will become your sworn enemy, and you will start a menstrual cycle. For some girls, puberty is scary at first, but it doesn't need to be. Even the hormone-driven mood swings can be managed by taking good care of yourself—eating right, exercising, staying hydrated, and getting enough sleep. The good news about puberty is that it's an important step in you becoming a woman. Nobody stays forever young, except plastic surgery celebrities who live in their own kind of make-believe. Middle school is no fairy tale, and puberty isn't the horror movie some make it out to be. What can you do to make the most of this awkward yet important stage of life? Don't fight it. Embrace the changes and take care of yourself. Just as caterpillars become butterflies, girls become women. The transformation can feel confining and uncomfortable, but the end result is beautiful.

Pop Quiz

Q: How old are most girls when they begin puberty?

A: First signs of puberty in girls usually start between the ages of 8 and 13 years old.

RAISE YOUR HAND

*O*oh, ooh, ooh, call on me. Call on me. I know it. I know this one. I know. Over here. Right here. Me, me, me. Call on MEEEE!!!!!!"

There you are, waving your arms around, hands raised high, and you know the teacher can hear you begging for a chance to be heard. But nooooo. They call on the kid sitting over there all calm, hand barely raised over their head. That or the teacher calls on the kid who's not even raising their hand. What? Why? Well, let's see if you know the answer to this one, smart girl. Are you pushy? Do you ever blurt out the answer? Do you have an expert opinion for every question the teacher asks? Or let's consider the opposite. Do you hide in the back of class and avoid all contact with the teacher? When you are asked a question, do you shrug it off and mumble, "I dunno . . ."?

Let's go with this. It's a good idea to raise your hand from time to time, when you know the answer. But it's never good to be a know-it-all, all the time. Girls who try to sit all quiet hoping not to be noticed will eventually be asked to speak up. Chances are the one time the teacher does volunteer you to share is the exact time you don't know what the teacher is talking about. Your best plan is to raise your hand with an answer when you know the answer, at least once a day. It's not hard. Simply lift your hand over your head and make eye contact with the teacher. When they call on you, share what you know or ask a good question to help you learn more. It's also good to raise your hand to ask good questions every now and then. If you don't get what the teacher is teaching, put that hand up and ask a question. Ask good questions and you will get good answers. Ask shallow questions and you can expect shallow answers. Ask no questions and you will get no answers.

How To . . .
Fake an Answer

> ***STEP 1***—Trick question! Your teacher already knows the answer to the question they just asked. Do you really think they are new to this? Seriously, they are a credentialed pro and you're just trying to fake it. Nice try.

READING FOR FUN

Girls who read can go anywhere, do anything, and be anyone they choose. Readers transport through time from ancient days to futuristic fantasies. Readers have seen the glory of a hero's adventure and the intrigue of true mystery. Readers have looked out over a sea of adoring fans chanting their name and stood alone against the wrath of an enemy determined to destroy. Readers fly on the backs of dragons and explore the depths of space. Readers are the first to discover and the last to abandon their imagination. Girls who read can travel the world, save the universe, and live a thousand lives before finishing middle school. Girls who never read will live only once.

"A book is like a garden, carried in the pocket."

—Chinese Proverb

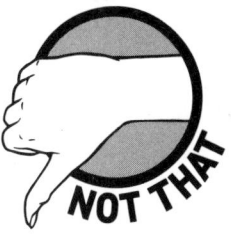

READING FOR SCHOOL

*O*kay, here's the situation. Your homework this weekend is to read chapters 8 and 9 in your world history book. On Monday morning there will be a closed-book test worth 10% of your final grade. What will you do? If you're thinking it's a good plan to read the chapters and take notes about the important parts, then you are setting yourself up for success come test time. If you are thinking reading is dumb and taking notes is a waste of time because there are no important parts, um . . . good luck with that. A good plan is to finish the assigned reading before the assigned time. How you do this is up to you, but do plan your reading and work your plan. Some girls like to just "get it done" all at once. Others prefer to read for a few minutes here, a few minutes there, and then push through with an hour of no interruptions and good note taking. Try a few strategies until you find the one that helps the reading stick with you. Remember, just pushing through the words does you no good if you can't recall what they said. You never know, you might just read something new and cool enough to remember after the test.

Ask a Middle School Survivor

Q: What happens when I don't do the summer reading the middle school assigns?

A: The school will mark it down as a bad grade. I really don't think you want to start the year off in trouble. Summer reading is one of the first grades of the year, so you'll want to do your very best.

Macy S., from North Carolina

REPORT CARDS

*R*eport cards are a lot like sports scores. How a team performs on the field or court shows up on the scoreboard without bias. That means no coach, official, or fan can just toss up or take off points to make a team look better or worse than they actually performed. The same is true about your report card. Teachers can't just "give" you a good or bad grade. What they post in report cards is an accounting of how you performed in their class. Basically, you did the work and they kept the score. If you want to keep score too, you can. In fact, a good game plan includes you knowing how well you are doing in each class day to day. Most middle schools give you access to an online grade book where you and your parents can see what assignments are handed in, which are missing, the grades you've earned, test scores, and extra credit points. You'll be able to see, track, and predict what your score/grade will be on report card day. This way you can own your own grades and not just wait for the end of the game to learn the score.

To Do in Middle School:

✓ Make AB Honor Roll.

RESPECT UPPERCLASSMEN

*F*ear and respect are two different things. You have no need to fear the students in the grades above you. Yet, showing them respect is a must. The best advice is simply to treat your "elders" like you would want to be treated. Show them some respect by being polite and staying cool when they are around, and they are more likely to be good to you too.

Strange but True

In Tibet, sticking your tongue out is a greeting and a sign of respect. But to the Māori people of New Zealand, sticking out your tongue is part of the war chant, preceding battle.

SCHOOL PICTURES

*L*ook at the camera and smile. This is for the yearbook, not a mug shot. Posing for a school picture is nothing new to you. You've been doing it since you were in kindergarten. The difference now is that the picture captured in middle school will not just get mailed out to grandparents to be framed or hung on their fridge—that pic is also going into the yearbook. Come the end of the school year, that book will hold you forever captive between the two kids with last names alphabetically beside yours. So what is your plan for picture day? Besides wearing an outfit that is both cool and clean, keep these do's and don'ts in mind as you strike your pose.

Do—smile

Don't—pucker your lips like a duck

Do—tilt your head slightly

Don't—over-tilt your head

Do—try to look natural

Don't—try to look like nature

Really, it's up to you. It's not like people are going to keep that school picture forever. Oh wait, yes they will. Say cheese.

Looking Back

When your mom tells you what to wear on school picture day or to pull your hair back so she can see your face, it just proves she still cares. Truth is, you'll wear what you want. But don't forget, that's the pic everybody will see in the yearbook.

—Erica M., from Oregon

SHAVING

*R*aise your hand . . . now take a peek under your arm. Yes, check out your armpit. Is there hair starting to grow there? If so, it may be time to shave. If you live in other parts of the world shaving is pretty optional, and today some women in the US let their armpit and leg hair grow free. But if you aren't the type to let the armpit hair flow, you will need to take the time to shave. To help you avoid razor burn, nicks, or cuts, you can read specific how-to instructions on shaving in our other book, *The Girls' Guide to Conquering Life*. As you ponder your shaving choices, consider this famous quote said by Ms. Nowomanever: "I like shaving with a dull razor."

True Story

I shaved my legs for the first time when I was in 5th grade. I borrowed my mom's razor and, without asking, mowed down my leg hair. A few minutes later my legs were minus hair and plus a few razor-burn bumps and one bloody nick. When I showed my mom what I had done she wasn't very happy. Mom cried and said I was too young. Looking back, I should have asked my mom for help. I probably could have avoided the razor burn and blood, but my mom would probably still have cried.

—Erica Catherman

SHOWERING

*Y*ou know what really stinks about middle school? Middle schoolers. *FLASH!* That's the bright light of truth flipping the switch on. Now maybe you'll see that what might look clean doesn't always smell clean. And that includes you. But wait. There's more to smell in this story, and it's not all roses. Think about it. By the time a parent, teacher, friend, random weirdo, or pack of mean boys says you smell, how many other people noticed too? Only one person was brave, or socially insensitive, enough to say something. What can you do to avoid the embarrassment of being the stinky girl? Here's a good plan. It's time to start showering. Every day! In fact, showering daily is part of growing up. An unwashed middle school body can quickly become encased in a dingy layer of dirt, sweat, makeup, and tweenage hormones. Soap, shampoo, water, and a clean towel are the only true way to refresh your natural self and keep people from pinching their noses when you walk their way.

Pop Quiz

Why does using soap when washing work?
  (A) Magic.
  (B) Soap allows insoluble particles to become soluble in water so they can then be rinsed away.
  (C) Because my mom says so.
  (D) Both A & C.

Answer: (B) Soap allows insoluble particles to become soluble in water so they can then be rinsed away.

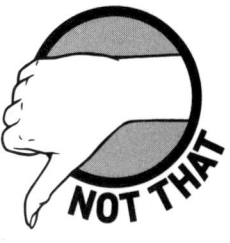

SIBLINGS

Older, younger, twins, half, or step, the classification of relation and age range between you and your sibling(s) matters little. The fact is, by the time you are in middle school, you'll have spent about 33% of your spare time with your siblings. That means you have hung out with your stinking brother or crazy sister more than with your friends, teachers, parents, or even by yourself.[17] The quality of the time you spend together probably ranges from hugs to thugs. One minute you are best friends, the next mortal enemies, and then back to good by dinner. You share looks and a last name, a branch on the family tree, and maybe even a room in the house. The most important thing about dealing with your siblings is learning that as you grow older, they aren't going to be important people in your life—they'll be some of the *most important* people in your life.

True OR False?

Some twins can be the same and the opposite at the same time.

True. Some twins are mirror twins. This means they have the same physical features but on opposite sides of their body. If one twin is right-handed, the other is left. Some mirror twins can even have mirror organs. One's heart is on the left and their twin's heart is on the right. Even their skeletal features can be reversed.[18]

SICK DAYS

Sick or not sick? That is the question. If you are, stay home. Nobody at school needs to be exposed to your clammy hands and pre-puke face. If you're not really feeling bad, don't lick your palms or whine about fake symptoms in an attempt to avoid some test you "don't feel good" about taking. Believe it or not, you have a limited number of sick days before passing a class or grade level becomes a real headache. When you do miss school for a day or two after yacking into the porcelain throne, bring a parent's or doctor's note to the office with an explanation of your absence. And to all you actors out there, keep this fun fact in mind: Once you've faked sick a few times, nothing short of barfing up a lung will convince people you really do need bed rest.

True Story

THE KISSING DISEASE

The 8th grade was the best two years of my middle school life. Seriously, I repeated the 8th grade because I'd been absent for two months, sick with mononucleosis. This energy-draining illness is also known by the shortened title "mono" and its nickname favored by my friends, the "kissing" disease. I liked my buddy's nonclinical diagnosis the best because it cast me as the one and only guy in our group of friends who had actually kissed a girl. (She would have been a sick girl, but a girl with willing lips nonetheless.) The problem was, I had no idea how I acquired the illness. My lips had no puckering experience, and in fact I would not kiss a girl for another year, at least.

—Jonathan Catherman

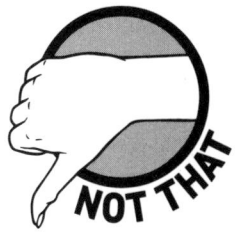

SKIPPING SCHOOL

What's the big deal? It's not like skipping school is illegal or anything. Well, actually . . . it is. Skipping school is legally called *truancy*, and truancy is illegal for middle school students. Decide not to come to school and you'll rack up an unexcused absence. Unexcused absences add up to makeups, including detention, Saturday school, summer school, and even fines issued to your parents. "Yeah, but school takes up so much time and I never really learn anything anyway," you say. Okay, smart girl, let's do the math and see what you know.

There are 365 days in a year, totaling 8,760 hours. The average student goes to school for about 6½ hours a day, 180 days a year. That totals out to about 1,170 hours per year in school. On average you'll sleep 7 hours a day,[19] totaling 2,555 hours a year. Nine hours a day will be connected to media,[20] ticking up to around 3,285 digital hours per year. You'll spend about 30 minutes a day in the bathroom, flushing away 182 hours a year. Now, if you've been keeping track, that leaves you with about 1,568 hours per year to do whatever you do in addition to going to school. So let's be honest here. With all those media minutes you probably spent multitasking while doing other things, you really have more "free time" than expected. It's basic math. Skipping school is illegal and doesn't add up to be a very valuable way to spend your time. Then again, smart girls like you who go to school know this because you've learned how to do the math.

Just Joking

Grandma: "Keep your voice down! The caller ID says it's your school. Must be because I let you skip today!"

Girl: "Don't answer. I told them I was attending your funeral!"

SOCIAL MEDIA

*M*uch *Ado About Nothing* is a play penned by William Shakespeare back in the way late 1500s. It's still popular today with middle school English teachers, so you may be reading it soon. The word *ado* means trouble or difficulty, and that's what the play is all about. Much of the ado in the play comes from a few handwritten letters that cause confusion, gossip, and misdeeds to spread quickly. If Shakespeare were writing the play today, he might exchange those handwritten letters with modern-day social media posts. Seems realistic, considering most people's social media posts are much *to-do* about nothing and easily cause much *ado* about nothing. Think of the time we spend paying attention to what took somebody next to no time to post. Here's a simple Shakespeare-approved line worth memorizing. It may just keep you out of much ado in future social media posts: "Not everyone needs to know everything about you."

True OR False?

Internet Addiction Disorder (IAD) affects up to 8.2% of the population in the US and Europe.

True. Many teenagers use social media and believe it's an important part of their lives. Yet some can get addicted to social media, causing their virtual life to negatively affect their real-world relationships and responsibilities. As powerful as alcohol and drug addiction is, IAD includes social media addiction as a real thing, which may require professional intervention.[21]

*I*n middle school you'll have your first opportunity to play on a school sports team. Some of the girls who show up for tryouts will have played in rec leagues for years, while others are giving the game their first shot. There is no guarantee the girl with more experience will make the team. Coaches are looking for team members who want to play, are teachable, and are willing to work hard to get better. Sure, raw talent is good, but ask any seasoned pro and they'll tell you exactly what it takes to win: "Hard work beats talent when talent doesn't work hard." So get out there and run, jump, shoot, hit, throw, flip, spike, and sweat your guts out. Make the team, and you can expect to win some games and lose some. What matters most in sports is not the ranking of your team, size of the trophies, or who scores the most points. What matters most is how you play the game as a TEAM. Together Everyone Achieves More. Also, you have a good time!

Pop Quiz

When were the first Olympic Games held on the plains of Olympia?

(A) 1910

(B) 1896

(C) 776 BC

Answer: (C) 776 BC. "The first ancient Olympic Games can be traced back to 776 BC. They were dedicated to the Olympian gods and were staged on the ancient plains of Olympia. They continued for nearly 12 centuries until Emperor Theodosius decreed in AD 393 that all such 'pagan cults' be banned."[22]

STEALING

Girl #1: "Finders keepers, losers weepers."

Girl #2: "Yeah, but you found those headphones inside my backpack."

Girl #1: "Don't try to confuse things with a technicality."

Isn't it interesting how "finders keepers" seems to always work in favor of the "finder"? Then when something of theirs gets "borrowed," they feel horribly wronged and believe the entire world is out to get them. Seriously, girl? There are no five-finger discounts in middle school or beyond. Seeing something you want and just taking it is stealing. We have a law here on planet Earth that basically says, "Thou shalt not steal." Also known as theft, robbery, lifting, forced sharing, or borrowing without permission, stealing is stealing. But why do some students feel so entitled to "claim" other people's stuff? Because they lack personal integrity. When a girl has integrity, your stuff is safe around her because she too believes in doing the right thing, even when nobody's watching. Be that girl.

"Real integrity is doing the right thing, knowing that nobody's going to know whether you did it or not."[23]

—Oprah Winfrey

STUDYING

*T*oday is Monday. The test is on Friday. When will you study? The right answer is *A little bit each night*. The wrong answer is *Tomorrow*. It's easy to find at least 50 excuses for why today is not a good day to study. You're busy, tired, hungry, bored, brain-dead, or rebelling against the system. Besides, you'll just cram the night before and ace that test on Friday. Fail. Here are a few study tips from a professional brain scientist who knows a thing or two about how the mind of a middle school student works. If you want to ace the test, try these study strategies on for size:

1. **Break it up**—Turn your study sessions into mini-lessons. Don't try to memorize the names of all the state capitals in one sitting. Instead, learn a few every day over a few days. Be sure to review what you learned last before starting the next set.[24]

2. **Move around**—Try studying the same stuff in a different place next time. You are more likely to remember the name of the state capitals when you move from studying in the library to your kitchen table, to the backyard, or to the gym after basketball practice. This forces your brain to form new associations with the same information, and that makes your memory sticky.[25]

3. **Work it out**—Getting some aerobic exercise builds more than your muscles. Research shows that running a couple laps around the house or doing a few jumping jacks between study questions will improve your brain-processing speed.[26]

True OR False?

By sleeping with a book under your pillow, the information will infiltrate your brain while you dream.

False. That would be cool though . . . osmosis!

SUBSTITUTE TEACHERS

Students say lots of things about substitute teachers. Some of what they say is true. Most of it isn't.

"I hear we have Mrs. Green as a substitute in math today. My friend's sister's locker partner was in band class with a kid who says Mrs. Green is really nice and that she thinks homework should be illegal, so she never gives it. I'm going to love her."

"I hear we have Miss Smith as a substitute in PE today. My sister knows this kid who used to go to school here but moved last year and she said Miss Smith was a Marine Drill Sergeant and gives people detention if they can't do 50 push-ups. I hate her already."

"I hear we have Ms. Holly as a substitute in history today. I heard this 8th grader say twice she shows kung fu movies in class and keeps the ashes of her dead dog in the backseat of her car. She is so weird."

Before you believe everything you hear about a substitute teacher, consider giving them the same break you'd want them to give you. Instead of being quick to judge, try getting to know them a little bit first. You may be surprised to learn most substitute teachers are pretty normal people, doing a really tough job, for not much pay.

Just Joking

Walking through the hallways of her middle school, a principal saw a new substitute teacher standing outside his classroom with his forehead resting against a locker.

The principal heard the substitute mutter, "How did you get yourself into this?"

Knowing he was assigned to a difficult class, the principal tried to offer the substitute some support. "Are you okay?" she asked. "How can I help you?"

The substitute teacher lifted his head and replied, "I'll be fine as soon as I can get this kid out of his locker."

SWEARING

*T*here are 191 four-letter words in the English language that start with the letter *f*. Most are *fine*, yet a few are particularly *foul* and should *fail* to ever *flow from* your *face*. In its simplest *form* you'll *find* cursing, swearing, profanity, blasphemy, and vulgarity all *flop flat* and *fall* to the lowest *form* of spoken expression. President Abraham Lincoln once said that it's "better to remain silent and be thought a *fool* than to speak out and remove all doubt."[27] Sure, dropping a *fury* of "f-bombs" in a *free-flow furl* of *foul flak* is *fuel* for *fake fame from fain fans*, but in *fact*, it's never clever. Verbally shocking *folk* with the *fail* of *foul* language is like playing in traffic. It's guaranteed to get people's attention *fast*, but in the end, the *fool* will *feel* the greatest pain.

Just Joking

Why did the chicken go to ISS?

Because she was caught using fowl language.

TEACHERS

*R*ecent advancements in human research have discovered a remarkable fact about student and teacher interactions. When exposed to powerful doses of the positively charged element Hu+, teachers often absorb the contagious properties of kindness in high concentrations. Hu+ then reproduces rapidly in the exposed subject and is released again by reverse osmosis toward students in close proximity. This amazing finding may sound impossible, yet in test after test the evidence is conclusive. Put simply, when a student is nice to a teacher, the teacher will be nice back to the student. Often referred to as The Golden Rule experiment, you can test the method for yourself, on your teachers. Your findings could change the world as you know it.

Ask a Middle School Survivor

Q: Are teachers out to get you in middle school?

A: No. While teachers may seem mean at first, they're not. For example, when they assign homework, they are not trying to "be mean" on purpose. Homework is probably part of their lesson plan and it's supposed to help you. Besides, doing the work at home may be less pressure and more comfortable than trying to get it all done in class.

Kea D., from Georgia

TESTING

*T*ests are part of school—and life. You'll hear some middle school students say stuff like, "I'm good at math, just not at taking tests." Okay, let's compare this test-taking trouble to life outside the classroom. Can a soccer team's starting striker be good at kicking the ball, just not during the game? Or what if a musician claimed to be a great rapper, just not when performing? You would never go to a doctor who knows all about healing people but forgets what to do during surgery. The trick to how pros perform under pressure is similar to how you can set yourself up for test-taking success. The pros have performance strategies, and good students do too. A good strategy for doing your best on a test is to have a proven plan for your test prep, taking, and completion. Here's a tried-and-true plan for you.

Test prep
- Study well in advance of the test.
- Get a good night's sleep before the test.
- Eat a good breakfast and drink some water.

Test taking
- Listen to the teacher's instructions.
- Read each question or passage all the way through before answering.
- Answer the questions you know first.
- When you don't know an answer, eliminate options you think are wrong.

Test completion
- Use any time you have left to double-check your work.
- Make sure your name is on the test.

Pop Quiz

Do the math:

$$111111111 \times 111111111$$

Answer: 12345678987654321

TEXTING

*O*n December 3, 1992, a 22-year-old test engineer named Neil sat at his computer and sent the first SMS text message to his friend Richard's phone. The message shared between the friends was a holiday greeting that read "Merry Christmas."[28] What started with one message in 1992 is now estimated to be 23 billion messages sent per day. That's over 16 million messages per minute. This means there's no escaping the short messages, and that can be a problem for you in middle school. Here's why. Splitting your attention between two or more tasks is called *multitasking*. Homework and texting is multitasking. Studying and texting is multitasking. Riding a bike and texting is multitasking. Walking and texting is multitasking. The problem is, our brains can't do either activity well when we try to do two tasks at once. When students try multitasking while doing schoolwork, they are splitting their attention. The quality of their learning gets really shallow. Students remember less and have trouble linking their learning to where it can be used in life. That, and we tend to run into things while texting and moving. Walking, riding, or driving and texting don't mix well. The same goes for texting and schoolwork. To get the most out of your reading, homework, and study time, you'll need to put the phone away. Your friends may wonder where you are for an hour, but your brain and body will thank you for a lifetime.

How To . . .
Lose Your Cell Phone to a Teacher in 5 Steps or Less

STEP 1—Sneak a text message in class.

STEP 2—Act surprised when the teacher sees you.

STEP 3—Deny sending a text message.

STEP 4—Claim your freedom of speech rights are being violated.

STEP 5—Hand over your cell phone.

TRACK THE TEACHER

*T*racking your teacher does not mean identifying their footprints and trailing them through the school's habitat and into the staff lounge. That's called *stalking*. Stalking is illegal and creepy. Stalking a teacher would probably get you suspended. Tracking your teacher is perfectly legal and helps keep you on the teacher's good list. To track your teacher, simply look at them when they are talking. If they move from one side of the class to the other, you keep watching them as they go. Hence, you track their progress through the lesson they are teaching.

Strange but True

People get paid to read body language. Experts in reading people's body language can make a living teaching their skills at seminars or working with police departments to determine by a suspect's body language whether they are lying.

TRASH

somebody gets paid to pick this up." That's what some girls think when they leave their trash behind instead of tossing it away. They walk off expecting somebody else to clean up after them like they employ a personal staff of merry maids. Seriously?! Technically, that's called *littering*. It's also called rude, selfish, and lazy, and it's a totally rotten thing to do. What if this was their house? More specifically, what if people left litter behind in your bedroom? Out of sight, out of mind . . . right? No way! You would strongly refuse (not be willing) to let other people's refuse (trash) pile up for you to pick up. The same rule applies at school. Toss your rubbish, and when it does fall short of the garbage/recycling can, own your litter recovery and leave no trash behind.

Just Joking

Why was the cafeteria trash can so sad?

He just got dumped.

VOICE VOLUME

*H*ere's a quick vocal lesson for beginners. Sound is measured in units of frequency called *hertz* (Hz). The hertz of a woman's voice ranges between 165 and 255, while a man's words measure between 85 and 155 Hz. The result is, women's voices sound higher than men's. No duh, right? But wait. Check out the vocal range of the typical kid entering middle school. The pre-puberty voices of both girls and guys wave in at 250 to 300 Hz! Add this high-pitched truth to the odd fact that kids' lung pressure is 50–60% higher than adults and what do you get? The answer isn't quiet.

Yet there are ways you can make your voice sound more mature. First, when in large groups, quiet down. The combined audio adrenaline of a class talking all at once can be high-pitched enough to make dogs howl and stress a teacher out to the breaking point of assigning extra home-work. Second, when you are called on in class, speak up. The class needs to hear your answer, and when you speak clearly and calmly, your voice is less likely to rise, peak, or sound flustered. In other words, your hertz will sound more mature.

True OR False?

The smallest bone in the human body is located in your ear.

True. The stapes is the smallest of three tiny bones in the middle ear that convey sound from the outer ear to the inner ear.

Volume

Volume

WRITING PAPERS

*H*andwritten or typed out, every good paper is drafted in steps.

STEP 1—Choose the topic. If the teacher assigns you the topic, then that step was easy.

STEP 2—Research information. This can be done online or in those ancient texts known as books. Either way, use only credible sources that are fact, not fan fiction.

STEP 3—Draft an outline. What are general ideas you want the beginning, middle, and end of your paper to say? How many points will you make along the way?

STEP 4—Organize your notes. You'll need information and notes on each of your main points.

STEP 5—Write a first draft. Don't worry about too much editing here. Just get your thoughts down in an organized way.

STEP 6—Edit the paper. Do your best to make sure what you are writing makes sense and flows well. Check for correct spelling and grammar.

STEP 7—Have somebody else edit the paper. Be open to suggestions and be willing to make any needed changes.

STEP 8—Prepare the final work. Format your paper exactly as the teacher assigned, and be sure to put your name on the top of the first page. Staple or bind the work as instructed, and hand that thing in, on time. Nice job, girl.

Pop Quiz

Q: Which animal can run the fastest: an elephant, a squirrel, or a mouse?

A: An elephant. Elephants can run up to 25 miles per hour.

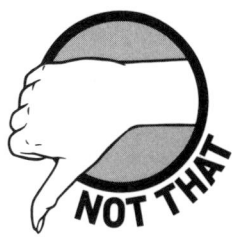

YEARBOOK

Captured forever on high-gloss paper, yearbooks are lasting proof of the best and many of the most embarrassing moments of middle school. Between the pictures of kids having fun, sports, clubs, and every student's portrait, your friends can sign and write their own thoughts. Here are a few of the least creative yet most common comments.

"Have a great summer." "Stay cool!" "Don't ever change." "Glad I got to know you." "Hope to see you next year." "Text me sometime."

Then there are the kids who put a little effort into what they write in their friends' yearbooks. Check out these original comments.

"If you like water, then you already like over 60% of me." "If crazy people could fly, our school would be an airport." "I love it when I start laughing and you start laughing at me so hard you gasp for breath. You should know most of the time I'm laughing it's because I just passed gas." "Any size pizza is a personal pizza, if you believe in yourself." "I waited 1,095 days to write this in your yearbook. Hi."

Write what you like, just remember people tend to keep yearbooks for the rest of their lives. Go ahead and get one, write in your friends', and feel free to laugh in the future at what everybody wrote, gas or not.

To Do in Middle School:

✓ Buy a yearbook.

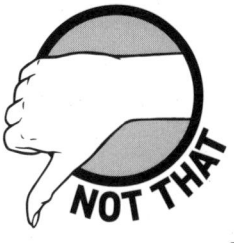

ZOMBIES

*B*elieved to be reanimated corpses capable of moving about in herds or in solo pursuit of brains to consume, zombies are feared by apocalypse preppers worldwide. The truth is, such beings are purely science fiction, unless you count some middle school students. Just watch the door of the school prior to first bell. There you will see students streaming in with glazed looks on their faces, hair matted, legs dragging, and drool spilling from their mouths. They are zombies! Or are they? Perhaps a logical explanation for their mindless herdlike movements is a lack of sleep, poor nutrition, and the belief that the day holds no real value. So how do you combat such a virus?

The antidote to zombieness is not as rare as you may think. To protect yourself, follow this three-part zombie-vanquishing plan and spread the word to anyone who will listen. First, get 8+ hours of sleep every night. Second, eat a good breakfast every morning. Third, look for something new and cool to discover and develop in yourself every day. That's it. Zombies are not real, yet students who live nearly numb lives are. Think of it this way: If you're not learning, you're not living. So go make the best of everything, and be sure to fill your middle school brain with good stuff. This time of life only comes once, so make the most of each and every day.

Looking Back

Middle school was full of ups and downs, kind of like a roller coaster. But roller coasters are fun, right? Whether or not you like roller coasters, embrace the changes middle school and puberty bring. In the words of my younger brother, "Do what YOU do and be who YOU be." Meaning you don't need to be like everyone else: The world needs YOU. Find confidence in who you are and what you do. Embrace your changes and allow yourself to grow into the woman YOU were intended to be. Be strong, kind, brave, and humble, and courageously adventure on—conquering every step of the way.

—Erica Catherman

RIDDLE ME THIS

1. A rooster sitting on the peak of a barn roof lays an egg. The peak of the barn roof faces north and south. It is the longest day of the year and the sun is directly overhead. Which way will the egg roll?

2. What do you fill with empty hands?

3. What goes around the world and stays in a corner?

4. What has one foot on the right, one on the left, and one in the middle?

5. What comes once in a minute, twice in a moment, and never in a thousand years?

6. Two mothers and their two daughters go shopping together. They each buy one bag to take home with them. They do not lose any bags, and yet when they arrive at home they only have three bags. How can this be?

7. You're a bus driver. At the first stop 4 people get on. At the second stop 8 people get on, at the third stop 2 people get off, and at the fourth stop everyone gets off. The question is, what color are the bus driver's eyes?

8. A sheriff rode into a small western town on Friday. She stayed two nights and left on Friday. How could that be?

9. What belongs to you but is used more by others?

10. I'm light as a feather, yet the strongest man can't hold me for more than 5 minutes. What am I?

11. Can you name three consecutive days without using the words *Wednesday*, *Friday*, and *Sunday*?

6. There are just three people: A grandmother, her daughter, and her granddaughter. 7. The same as yours; you're the bus driver. 8. Her horse's name is Friday. 9. Your name 10. Breath 11. Yesterday, today, and tomorrow.

212 .... Riddle Me This

12. What runs but never walks, often murmurs, never talks, has a bed but never sleeps, has a mouth but never eats?

13. They come out at night without being called and are lost in the day without being stolen. What are they?

14. The more you take, the more you leave behind. What am I?

15. What has a head and a tail but no legs?

16. What do you call a lemon that hits the floor?

17. What has six faces but doesn't wear makeup and also has 21 eyes but can't see?

18. What does a snow person like to eat for breakfast?

19. Why did the scarecrow win so many awards?

20. What did the softball glove say to the softball?

12. A river 13. Stars 14. Footsteps 15. A penny 16. A lemon drop 17. A die (dice) 18. Frosted Flakes 19. She was "out standing" in her field! 20. Catch you later.

21. Where do TVs go on vacation?

22. You can see me in water, but I never get wet. What am I?

23. What has cities but no houses, lakes but no water, and forests but no trees?

24. I have keys but no locks. I have space but no room. You can enter but can't go outside. What am I?

25. It's been around for millions of years, but it's no more than a month old. What is it?

26. What building has the most stories?

27. I am the only organ that named myself. What am I?

28. What kind of coat can only be put on wet?

29. Anthony's mom has four children. Her first child is a girl named April. Her second child is a girl named May. Her third child is also a girl and her name is June. What is the name of her fourth child?

21. Faraway, remote places 22. A reflection 23. A map
24. A keyboard 25. The moon 26. A library 27. The brain
28. A coat of paint 29. Anthony

30. Forward I am heavy. Backward I am not. What am I?

31. What has hands but no feet, a face but no eyes, tells but does not talk?

32. I never was. I am always to be. No one has ever seen me, nor ever will. Yet, all expect me. What am I?

33. What goes up and down stairs without moving?

34. Many have heard me, but no one has seen me, and I will not speak back until spoken to. What am I?

35. A window cleaner is cleaning a window on the top floor of a 25-floor skyscraper when, suddenly, he slips and falls! He has no safety equipment and nothing to soften his fall, yet he is not hurt. How can this be?

36. What superhero is the best softball player?

37. Mr. and Mrs. Smith have seven daughters. If each daughter has a brother, how many children do Mr. and Mrs. Smith have?

37. Eight

35. He is cleaning the inside of the window. 36. Batwoman

30. Ton 31. A clock 32. Tomorrow 33. A carpet 34. An echo

38. Spell "ghost" out loud. Then spell "most" out loud. Then spell "roast" out loud. What do you put in a toaster?

39. I know a word; six letters it contains. And yet if you take one away, twelve is what remains.

40. Which vehicle is spelled the same forward and backward?

41. When you write this time of day in capital letters it is the same forward, backward, and upside down. What time is it?

42. What word looks the same upside down and backward?

43. What is a seven-letter word containing thousands of letters?

44. I'm tall when I'm young and short when I'm old. What am I?

45. What body part is pronounced as one letter but written with three, only two different letters are used?

43. Mailbox 44. Candle 45. Eye
39. Dozen(s) 40. Racecar 41. NOON 42. SWIMS
38. Bread. (Most people will answer "toast.")

216   Riddle Me This

You'll need a calculator for the next three:

46. **Think of a number.**

    Key it into the calculator.

    Double it.

    Add 10.

    Halve it.

    Subtract the number you started with.

    What number are you left with?

47. **Key in the first 3 numbers of your phone number. (NOT your area code.)**

    Multiply by 80.

    Add 1.

    Multiply by 250.

    Add the last 4 digits of your phone number.

    Add the last 4 digits of your phone number again.

    Subtract 250.

    Divide the number by 2.

    Recognize the number?

48. **How much dirt is in a hole that's 4 feet wide, 4 feet long, and 4 feet deep?**

46. 5 47. It's your phone number. 48. None. There is no dirt in a hole. All the dirt has been removed. The calculator was only a distraction.

This is a trick question you will have to ask somebody else, because it only works when said out loud:

Ask, "There are six teacups on a table. If one falls off, how many are left on the table?"

Answer: Five. (They will say "59" . . . because they heard you say "60 cups." But you actually said, "Six teacups.")

NOTES

1. Edward Schor, ed., *Caring for Your School-Age Child: Ages 5 to 12*, the American Academy of Pediatrics (New York: Bantam, 2004).

2. Jonathan Catherman, *The Manual to Manhood* (Grand Rapids: Revell, 2014), 100.

3. Anne Klein, http://anneklein.com/then/.

4. This research, which was conducted by the German Society of Ophthalmology, was reviewed in "Women Cry More than Men and for Longer, Study Finds," *The Telegraph*, October 15, 2009, http://www.telegraph.co.uk/news/newstopics/howaboutthat/6334107 /Women-cry-more-than-men-and-for-longer-study-finds.html.

5. "8 Fascinating Facts about Tears," Berkeleywellness.com, http://www.berkeleywellness .com/self-care/preventive-care/slideshow/8-fascinating-facts-about-tears#.

6. Sameer Hinduja and Justin W. Patchin, *State Cyberbullying Laws*, Cyberbullying Research Center, Cyberbullying.org, updated January 2016, http://cyberbullying.org/Bully ing-and-Cyberbullying-Laws.pdf.

7. Jeff Kinney, *Diary of a Wimpy Kid* (New York: Amulet Books, 2007), 4.

8. Patty Jenkins, dir., *Wonder Woman*, Warner Bros., 2017.

9. Amy Poehler, Harvard Class of 2011 Commencement Speech, https://www.youtube .com/watch?v=7WvdxgGpNVU.

10. "Secrets of Human Hair Unlocked at the Natural History Museum in London," *The Guardian*, https://www.theguardian.com/uk/2004/may/27/sciencenews.research.

11. "Water, Sanitation, and Environmental-related Hygiene," Centers for Disease Control and Prevention, https://www.cdc.gov/healthywater/hygiene/index.html.

12. Information taken from Roy F. Baumeister and John Tierney, *Willpower* (New York: Penguin, 2011) and Kathleen Vohs, "Physical Order Produces Healthy Choices, Generosity, and Conventionality, Whereas Disorder Produces Creativity," *Psychological Science* 24, no. 9 (September. 2013).

13. Rachel Cruze, Instagram post, January 30, 2015.

14. "Longest Fingernails on a Pair of Hands Ever (Female)," Guinness World Records, http://www.guinnessworldrecords.com/records/hall-of-fame/lee-redmond-longest-finger nails-on-a-pair-of-hands.

15. John Medina, *Brain Rules* (Seattle, WA: Pear Press, 2008).

16. Emily Graham, "Principals Do the Darndest Things," PTO Today, http://www.pto today.com/pto-today-articles/article/614.

17. Jeffrey Kluger, "The New Science of Siblings," *Time*, July 10, 2006, http://content.time .com/time/magazine/article/0,9171,1209949-2,00.html.

18. "Mirror Twins: Fascinating Facts about Mirror Image Twins," *Twin Pregnancy and Beyond*, http://www.twin-pregnancy-and-beyond.com/mirror-twins.html.

19. "Sleep in Adolescents (13–18 Years Old)," Nationwide Children's Hospital, http://www.nationwidechildrens.org/sleep-in-adolescents.

20. Kelly Wallace, "Teens Spend a 'Mind-Boggling' 9 Hours a Day Using Media, Report Says," Nov. 3, 2015, https://www.cnn.com/2015/11/03/health/teens-tweens-media-screen-use-report/index.html.

21. A. Weinstein and M. Lejoyeux, "Internet Addiction or Excessive Internet Use," *American Journal of Drug and Alcohol Abuse* 36, no. 5 (August 2010): 277–83.

22. "History," Olympic.org, https://www.olympic.org/ancient-olympic-games/history-old.

23. Quoted by Elaine J. Hom, *Business News Daily Contributor*, March 6, 2013, https://www.businessnewsdaily.com/4080-business-profile-oprah-winfrey.html.

24. E. A. Kramár et al., "Synaptic Evidence for the Efficacy of Spaced Learning," NCBI, Proceedings of the National Academy of Sciences of the United States of America 109, no. 13 (March 2012): 1091–6490.

25. W. E. Hockley, "The Effects of Environmental Context on Recognition Memory and Claims of Remembering," *Journal of Experimental Psychology: Learning, Memory, and Cognition* 34, no. 6 (November 2008): 1412–29.

26. Henriette van Praag, "Exercise and the Brain: Something to Chew On," *Trends in Neuroscience* 32, no. 5 (2009): 283–90.

27. Fred R. Shapiro, "Abraham Lincoln," *The Yale Book of Quotations* (New Haven: Yale University Press, 2006), 466, italics added.

28. Victoria Shannon, "15 Years of Text Messages, a 'Cultural Phenomenon,'" *New York Times*, December 5, 2007, http://www.nytimes.com/2007/12/05/technology/05iht-sms.4.8603150.html.

Erica Catherman is the author of *The Girl's Guide to Conquering Life*. She has spent more than 20 years mentoring young women as a coach to middle school, high school, and college students. Committed to raising up the next generation to be kind, confident, and capable, Erica has served as a youth group leader, community volunteer, and advocate for gender equality in sports. She is a certified Yoga Alliance and Group Fitness instructor.

Jonathan Catherman is the author of the bestselling *The Manual to Manhood* and *The Manual to Middle School* and speaks worldwide about the principles and strengths that empower greatness in children, teens, and young adults.

The Cathermans live in North Carolina, where they work together to raise their family, which includes teenagers and a couple of big dogs. Learn more at www.TheCathermans.com.

CONNECT WITH

JONATHAN & ERICA CATHERMAN!

Ideationists, Consultants, Speakers, Authors

To learn more about the Cathermans'
speaking, consulting, and mentoring, visit

WWW.THECATHERMANS.COM

SKILLS MAKE YOU VALUABLE
CHARACTER MAKES YOU INVALUABLE

A mentoring program complete with curriculum, Club Kits, and impact studies that measure the growth of your MEN and WOMEN IN THE MAKING.

Visit www.1Mmentoring.org to learn more!

YOUR GO-TO RESOURCES
to be successful at life

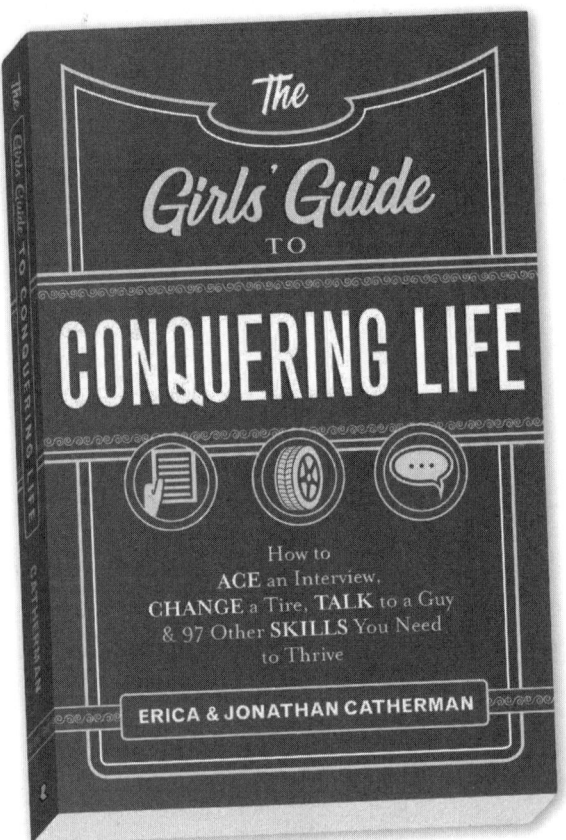

The Girls' Guide TO CONQUERING LIFE

How to ACE an Interview, CHANGE a Tire, TALK to a Guy & 97 Other SKILLS You Need to Thrive

ERICA & JONATHAN CATHERMAN

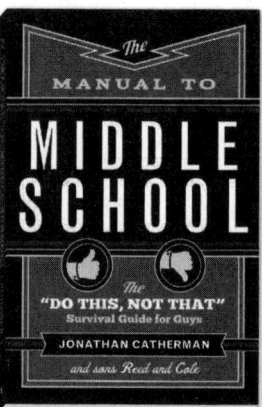

The MANUAL TO MIDDLE SCHOOL

The "DO THIS, NOT THAT" Survival Guide for Guys

JONATHAN CATHERMAN
and sons Reed and Cole

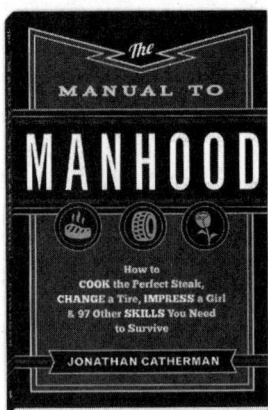

The MANUAL TO MANHOOD

How to COOK the Perfect Steak, CHANGE a Tire, IMPRESS a Girl & 97 Other SKILLS You Need to Survive

JONATHAN CATHERMAN

Revell
a division of Baker Publishing Group
www.RevellBooks.com

Available wherever books and ebooks are sold.